Updike's America

American University Studies

Series XXIV
American Literature

Vol. 2

PETER LANG
New York · Bern · Frankfurt am Main · Paris

Dilvo I. Ristoff

Updike's America

The Presence of Contemporary American History in John Updike's Rabbit Trilogy

PETER LANG
New York · Bern · Frankfurt am Main · Paris

Library of Congress Cataloging-in-Publication Data

Ristoff, Dilvo I.
  Updike's America.

  (American university studies. Series XXIV,
American literature ; vol. 2)
  Bibliography: p.
  Includes index.
  1. Updike, John. Rabbit, run. 2. Updike, John.
Rabbit redux. 3. Updike, John. Rabbit is rich.
4. Updike, John—Knowledge—History. 5. Historical
fiction, American—History and criticism. I. Title.
II. Series.
  PS3571.P4R337 1988   813'.54   87-22799
  ISBN 0-8204-0717-8
  ISSN 0895-0512

CIP-Titelaufnahme der Deutschen Bibliothek

Ristoff, Dilvo I.:
Updike's America : the presence of contempor-
ary American history in John Updike's Rabbit
trilogy / Dilvo I. Ristoff. – New York; Bern;
Frankfurt am Main; Paris: Lang, 1988.
  (American University Studies: Ser. 24,
  American Literature; Vol. 2)
  ISBN 0-8204-0717-8

NE: American University Studies / 24

Printed by Weihert-Druck GmbH, Darmstadt, West Germany

To
Maria and Clarissa

Acknowledgements

This study owes its existence to a number of people at the University of Southern California and at the Federal University of Santa Catarina. I would like to thank especially Professors Jay Martin, Ronald Gottesman, and Wesley Bjur for their encouragement, kindness, and wise counseling throughout the research. The support received from many of my colleagues at the Federal University of Santa Catarina can only be collectively acknowledged. Thank you. Finally, I would like to express my deepest gratitude to CAPES (COORDENACAO PARA O APERFEICOAMENTO DO PESSOAL DO ENSINO SUPERIOR), the Brazilian agency which provided the funds that made this study possible.

Dilvo I. Ristoff
Los Angeles, California—June 1987.

Table of Contents

Preface xi

Introduction 1

1   From Agent to Scene 11

2   The Domestic Rabbit 39

3   The Solid Citizen 75

4   The Hostage of Fortune 113

Conclusion 143

Bibliography 161

Index 171

Preface

I met John Updike on a cold Sunday morning, last December, at a street corner, close to his home in Beverly Farms, Massachusetts. When I introduced myself he asked with disbelief "Have you been standing here in the cold waiting for me to materialize?" A little earlier I had seen a huge crowd coming from church and going to church, so that one of the first questions I asked him was "Are you going to church?" "No," he answered, "I'm coming from church. I'm on my way to buy the newspaper." With all this Sunday morning religious atmosphere around me, and with Updike's strange description of himself as a spirit which could materialize, in my mind, the image of Rev. Eccles, Rev. Kruppenbach, Rev. Soupy, Rev. Tom Marshfield, and others immediately came to life. And so did a whole sphere of criticism on Updike's work, from the Hamiltons, through Edward Vargo, Rachael Burchard, Joyce Markle, Suzanne Uphaus, to Michael Novak. For a moment I thought that I had knocked at the wrong door and that I had better follow the roads already so smoothly paved by the established criticism. Perhaps it was all a parable, as the Hamiltons want it! Perhaps Updike was telling us of "those aspects of earth which can speak to us of heaven;" perhaps Updike's main purpose was indeed to let us "see that, behind the shifting surface of the experiences life brings us, there is one constant question, which each one of us must answer for himself: Does the universe, blindly ruled by chance, run downward into death; or does it follow the commands of a Living God whose Will for it is life?" So that when Updike asked me which aspect of his fiction I was studying, I was not so sure if he would like what I had to tell him, and I was not very sure whether I should tell him. Added to all this ethereal atmosphere, I was well aware of Updike's dislike of critics and PhD students. I certainly had good reasons for feeling somewhat uneasy. In *Picked-up Pieces*, for instance, Updike talks about critics as those

who take "all those little congruences and arabesques you prepared with such anticipatory pleasure [and] gobble [them] up
[like] pigs at a pastry cart." I also had in mind Bech's stamp with
the reply "WRITE IT YOURSELF" to all letters coming from PhD
students. Although I had all this in mind and felt that somehow
I had my feet and my snout in the mud, I quickly told him about
my project.

"O, you're writing about *Buchanan Dying,* he said.

"No," I answered, "I'm writing about your use of history in
the Rabbit trilogy."

"Really?" He seemed somewhat surprised. Then he added,
"Yes, I guess there is a lot of history there, but I always thought
of *Buchanan* as the most obviously history-oriented book."

I saw no reason to disagree.

"Well, I took you by the word. You said in an interview that
there is more history in your fiction than in history books. I
believed you."

"Did I say that?" He smiled.

"Believe me," I said, "your books taught me a lot about
America."

He was obviously flattered. "O, but it is just a one man's
view," he said.

"But a very good one, a very (I emphasized the very) good
one indeed."

We went into the drugstore. He bought the Boston Globe and
we drove, past a lake in the woods, to his home, a huge white
mansion surrounded with Greek columns, up on a hill, over-
looking the Atlantic Ocean, not far from the witches of Salem. I
told him that, if he didn't mind it, I would love to take some
pictures of his house, that my students would not believe I had
been there if I had nothing to show them.

"They would probably want me on it," he volunteered.

And that came to be the most important moment of my trip
to New England. Without realizing it, I took a picture which
became emblematic of the contents of this volume. The picture
shows John Updike standing in front of his house (the future
House of the Seven Gables?) holding a newspaper — the Sunday

Globe—in his hands. Only after I had arrived home and seen the picture did I realize that that picture symbolized everything I was trying to do, namely, to show that Updike has to be "seen" with a newspaper in his hand. The newspaper in all its polyphony was the very symbol of the scene I had been trying to recover. The picture was telling me that Updike was volunteering a contribution to my reading of his work.

At Harvard's Houghton Library, for the last ten days, I had seen, along with the novels' manuscripts, scraps, and erasures, evidence enough of Updike's scenic concerns and of his creative method. Among the coffee stains and other things, I had seen:

(a) blank spaces in the original manuscripts, in those spots where newsbroadcasts were meant to be added later. Only in later drafts were the blanks filled and the broadcasts added to the text. I have no authorization to reprint these pages, but they would certainly help to desacralize Updike's scenic concerns. Needless to say that he put a lot of research effort into it before he added the radio broadcasts to the final text. In my conversation with him, I casually asked him why he had made Prime-minister MacMillan and President Eisenhower meet in Gettysburg? "Wasn't it Gettysburg?" he asked surprised. When I told him that they had met in Camp David, he looked disappointed, as if I had told him he had not done his job properly. We talked for a while about it and I believe that in the end I did manage to convince him that Gettysburg works better than Camp David in the novel.

(b) I also saw newspaper clippings, with entire articles taken from the *Sunday Globe*. These articles were used by Updike to generate discussions, thoughts, images, etc. in the novels. A good example are the oil- crisis articles which were used in *Rabbit is Rich,* one article having probably become the source of the novel's wonderful first sentence—"Running out of gas"—that sentence which so effectively connects Harry's middle age dryness with America's energy crisis. Already in the first sentence, Harry is equated to America.

There are also clippings with the price of gold, silver, and other metals—information which became the basis for Harry's calculations of how much money he was making and how many Krugerrands he could buy.

(c) There are brochures from Toyota dealers, copies of *Automotive News*—all material which became sort of essential for Updike's description and discussion of Rabbit's life at his Toyota agency. Not less important is the photocopy of the manual of the used-car dealer, an entire book whose use in the novel I do not see any need to comment upon.

(d) Updike also added pictures, actual photographs, probably taken by himself, of buildings and streets in Reading, Pennsylvania—an obvious attempt to show that his Brewer stands for a real place where real people live.

(e) I also saw calendars and graphs with dates and corresponding events—material which was used to accompany the characters' journey in time, through a very specific year, month, day, an hour.

(f) Remarkable is also the map of the Kent State University Campus, the campus of the university which Rabbit's son, Nelson, attends, and also the University of the 1970 student demonstrations. That the reactionary Nelson should now in 1979 be a student at a university which nine years before was the scene of violent protests, only shows Updike's attempt to portray the present conservative mood of America against the comparatively revolutionary sixties. Updike did not only have the map of the campus's geography in front of him, but also the map of the campus's political atmosphere.

(g) Updike's concern with reproducing scenic details with realistic accuracy is probably the explanation why Daniel Starer wrote him a letter offering him his services. Starting March 25, 1980, he writes, he can offer John Updike research service full-time, at 8$ an hour or at $60 a day. The tone of the letter indicates that he had done research for Updike before, although I was unable to confirm this information. What this information would tell us is that Updike takes his scenic concerns very seriously indeed. His view is that the writer's role is not only to transcribe reality but to transcribe it as faithfully as possible, even if to do so one needs the help of a professional.

(h) And, finally, among the multitude of scraps which are neatly kept in various folders, one finds church programs and invitations, old checkbooks covered with scribbles, and even, hospital bills. That Updike chose to preserve these scraps for posterity has to do not only with their direct use in the novels but also with his belief, despite of what he says against pig-critics, that this material is important for reconstituting the scene in which his work was produced.

It would be too lengthy and too tiresome to go on enumerating the material on which Updike clearly relied for the writing of his novels. The totality of the scene can obviously never be recaptured, but Updike's manuscripts at the Houghton Library offer a whole range of national, international, and local events (from politics to economics to religion to crime to the "daily doings of ordinary people") upon which Rabbit has planted his roots and to which he is forced to react. Updike's declaration that man is always born into one system or another proves to be a conviction. The scene is something a man is born into and which he cannot escape. And the scene is where and why Rabbit comes to life, for the scene, in its complexity, is an event. Jorge Luiz Borges once said that his father's library was the most important event in his life. For Rabbit, the scene America is the most important event of his life. Without America Rabbit is inconceivable. Without this scene which, like Borges's library, becomes act or event, Rabbit's life would lose its interest and its flavor. Inextricably attached to the American scene, to its events, to its mood, to its concerns, Rabbit gains life and will remain alive but, above all, he will remain American to the extreme.

Morris Dickstein in his book *Gates of Eden* (1977) refers to this technique of Updike, implying that it is so scene-centered that any writer can produce a Comedie Humaine just by finding "another corner of reality to portray," as long as he has energy enough. This technique, argues Dickstein, probably explains why writers like Updike and Joyce Carol Oates are so prolific. This is just an en-passent remark made by Dickstein, but it argues my point that there is a real scene out there which the Updike books can, better than any other, help us recapture. The

American scene, in all its polyphony and diversity, is Updike's muse. To this scene which writes his texts, he has added the energy of a horse, the discipline of a seminarist, and the intellectual refinement of a Harvard "suma-cum- laude" student.

During my meeting with Updike I told him that now, after having spent nearly ten days at the Houghton library, drowned in his manuscripts, I could understand better why I had never become a fiction writer. He wanted to know why.

"Because it is too much work," I said.

"Well," he said, half smiling, half serious, "you don't do it all at once. You do a little bit every day."

This daily work routine shows that Updike does see himself less as a romantic genius and more as a mediating link between the text of reality and the text on the page. As he says in an article entitled "The Artist and his Audience," his view of art is "rather fatalistic and deterministic. What does this view do to the creative imagination?" He answers: "the creative imagination, I would say, functions with a certain indispensable innocence within its implacable context." Thus, he concludes: "An art form does not determine itself from abstract or intrinsic causes; it is shaped by the technology and appetite of the time." The final implication is that "more and more the writer thinks of himself as an instrument, a means whereby a time and a place—[what I term scene]—make their mark." He sees himself, therefore, as a translator trying to communicate with his audience and trying to please his audience.

And it is this view of art as having primarily a communicative function, along with the creative imagination's desire to please, that makes Updike share with his audience that which is most precious to him and, which, because he views them as precious, he believes his audience ought to hear. And for Updike painting is one the most precious activities in life. His past experience as a cartoonist and painter seems to have had a definite influence over his attitudes as a writer. As he himself admits, "[his] writing tends...to be pictorial, not only in its groping for visual precision but in the way books are conceived, as objects in space, with events and persons composed within them like shapes on a canvas." And what Updike cherishes most is to paint America, to recreate the scene into which he was born and into which every American is born. The scene is rich in contradictions and any honest portrayal will include them and allow them to develop. Thus, we find in the Rabbit novels, not only Rabbit's strength, his honesty, his pragmatism, and sense of guilt, but also his weaknesses, his militarism, his racism, his immaturity, his nationalism, his selfishness. And if the scene is to be properly portrayed, the ideological spectrum has to appear with a reasonable degree of plausibility in order to be believable. Thus, we have different ideologies being developed to such a degree that an actual subversion of truth, a sort of Bahktinian carnivalization, takes place. Updike has defined this "subversiveness" as the yes/but quality of his fiction, but one should add that this quality is the very refusal to absolutize the world, a terminant refusal to place the truth in the hands of a Rabbit, of an Eccles, of a Skeeter, of a Jill, of a Stavros, of a Mr. Springer, or whoever. The truth has no fixed place and no permanent owner; it can only be found in the text's capacity to desacralize authority and in its contribution to our understanding of the complexity of America.

This is, then, where I believe my contribution to the Updike scholarship comes in. What I argue is that

(a) Updike's fiction is born into an out of a scene which is place-specific and time-specific and which, therefore, is obsessively referential in nature.

(b) Updike's fiction, because of its referentiality, reflects primarily a world which, despite its frequent religious themes, expresses human relationships whose explanations are primarily at the realm of the social rather than of the mystic.

(c) the social relations frequently express conflicts and moods which are generated by history, usually by topical events of national and international repercussion, e.g., the cold war atmosphere, the Korean War, the Vietnam War, the Civil Rights movement, the moon landing, the Ted Kennedy accident, the oil crisis, the hostage crisis, the Toyota invasion, the Iranian revolution, etc.

(d) the Rabbit trilgoy can be read with a scene-centered approach, consistently, without having to change Rabbit's fundamental characteristics, that is from a rebel without a cause in the fifties to a an establishment citizen in the sixties and seventies. My argument is that the Domestic Rabbit of the fifties is the solid citizen of the sixties and the Rotary Club member of the seventies, and that throughout the three decades he expresses the same fundamental characteristics of the middle American Radical, as indicated by Donald I. Warren in his book called *The Radical Center* (1976). These characteristics are militarism, racism, nationalism, pragmatism, religiosity, and authoritarianism.

(e) a scene-centered approach helps us to see more clearly that Rabbit stands for those forces which carry America and with which Rabbit tends to identify. Rabbit invariably identifies with the President in office, irregardless of political party and no matter what the critics tell him. But because he always identifies himself even better with presidents who are already breathing their last breath or are out of office, he is somehow always trying to recover a scene that is no more. That he identifies better with Carter than he does with Nixon, for example, is also the explanation for his greater sense of having achieved total integration with the system at last. The comedy of *Rabbit is Rich* stems from the process of adaptation of little kids to the world of Rotary Club members. It is also the comedy of a man trying to learn to live with wealth, e.g., "what's the use of being rich if you don't live like one?" or "What's the use of being rich if you feel guilty when buying a can of cashew nuts?" The tragedy in *Rabbit is Rich* is postponed, but it is there nonetheless. It is in Rabbit's incapacity to pay attention to the vague uneasiness and to the nightmarish dreams which tell him that he, the nationalist, the all-American, is rich because of the Japanese, the Arabs, the foreign cars he sells, and the lack of confidence which plagues the country.

Finally, (f), I argue that the historical material is not ancillary but essential for a full appreciation of Updike's sequel. A reading of the novels without a recognition of the appropriation of the historical by the fictional characters will necessarily fail to capture the complexity and beauty of the social, economic, and political universe Updike so carefully portrays. Many critics recognize the importance of the scene (e.g., Vaughn, Detweiler, Greiner, even the Hamiltons and Vargo) but they fail to show the actual integration of the scenic and historic into the fictional. The crux of my argument is then not only the need to restore referentiality, it is also to show the generative power of the referents, and to point to the inseparableness of fiction and history.

The picture of Updike holding the *The Boston Globe*, therefore, is a perfect symbol of this inseparableness of man and scene, or of the fictional character and the world he inhabits. After all, what is a newspaper if not a texturization of the marks of time and space on man and of the marks of man on time and space? What I try to do in the following discussion is to show how Updike connects these various marks he has in his hands in order to reveal to us what I decided to call simply Updike's America, an America which is only a version, it is true, but a version which is rich, vivid, doubtlessly among the best examples of social fiction in the United States. If all that happens in this America is, as the Hamiltons want it, "governed by eternal laws and visited by divine grace" I do not know, and I do not see any reason to doubt it. It is all perfectly possible, but more visibly before us are the "laws" made by ministers of the church, businessmen, politicians, and the economy. I felt content exploring some of those. As Updike tells Bech: "the American style and landscape and impetus [are], by predetermination, his meat." I could not see why I should not, with all this meat, have a barbecue.

Introduction

"My fiction about the daily doings of ordinary
people has more history in it than history books,
just as there is more breathing history in
archaeology than in a list of declared wars and
changes of government"

(Picked-Up Pieces).

John Updike's concern with the use of history can be observed
in almost all of his fiction. Most of his novels and many of his
short stories can be placed with absolute precision in time and
space, either through direct references in the text or through
detailed descriptions of the context and its memorabilia. *Rabbit,
Run* (1960), *Rabbit Redux* (1971), and *Rabbit is Rich* (1981) are
among the best examples of this, almost obsessive, concern of
Updike with the integration of the historic into the fictional and
of the fictional into the historic. Not only do we know, for example, the exact year these novels start and end, but we also know
the exact month, the exact day, and almost the exact hour in
which the actions start unfolding and, in due course, end. The
same may be said about Updike's Brewer and Mount Judge,
towns which, with a quick survey of a Pennsylvania road map,
are unmistakably identified with Reading and Shillington,
where most of the actions of the Rabbit trilogy take place.

This concern with placing the stories so precisely in time and
space is Updike's open invitation to the audience to read, along
with the novels, a text which parallels and complements them,
becoming in the process so actively participant in the literary
text that to ignore it is not only difficult but impossible. Such is
the case with the novels of the Rabbit trilogy—all of them so
deeply rooted in history that a refusal to historicize them is also
a refusal to fully appreciate their quality.

Updike's work is based on the assumption that man is a creature of time and space and that in his "encounter [of] the reality
of experience," as Stephen Dedalus would put it, the "con-

science of [his] race" or of his countrymen is forged. Harry (Rabbit) Angstrom, the protagonist of the three Rabbit novels, is
precisely such a creature of time and space. Rabbit is Updike's
creation or, rather, recreation of the "conscience" of America, as
it presents itself in the life of a common American man at a very
specific moment in time. As Updike puts it in an interview to
Michael Sragow, there is no way of escaping the scene, for "you
are [always] born into one political contract or another."[1] The
Rabbit novels illustrate this view unequivocally.

The immediate implication of such an assumption is that
man's actions occur in direct relation to the reality of his environment, generating conflicts, creating tensions, determining
actions, shaping thoughts, establishing moods and fashions.
This does not mean that all individuality is lost and that man
has become a recorded reproduction of his environment. Such a
mechanistic interpretation would be impossible to sustain even
with the most naturalistic of novels, not to mention a sequel like
the Rabbit trilogy where the protagonist is constantly out of step
with his environment. Thus, the implication of Updike's
assumption means no more and no less than the affirmation that
the individual's existence in society is, by necessity, a social existence, and that the nature of the agent and the nature of scene
have to be intrinsically compatible, as Kenneth Burke argues in
his *A Grammar of Motives* (1945).[2] The "quality of agenthood"
which perforce permeates the scene is abstracted out of reality
and presented to us by Updike as being at one time individual
and social. In other words, the individual stands in relation to
society somewhat like the idiolect stands in relation to language—no one can absolutely deny its uniqueness or singularity, but even that uniqueness and singularity can only be
affirmed through its deviations from the common ground it
shares with language. Or, as Frederick Jameson puts it when
explaining the Sausserean thought: "in language the perception
of identity is the same as the perception of difference."[3] The
same happens with Updike's man—he is portrayed as retaining
a certain measure of individuality, but that individuality serves
mainly to reveal the broader social text with whose essentials he

is suffused, like a prisoner who with others shares a cell in "The Prison-House of Language." He may refuse to communicate, but if he chooses to communicate and when he does achieve communication, it is done on the basis of what he shares with others and not on his idiosyncrasies, although these may very well be revealed, or enhanced even, in the communicative process.

Harry Angstrom, the protagonist of the Rabbit novels, is typical of these fictional prisoners of the social text. His incapacity to escape as well as his capacity to engage in dialogue, to reproduce the collective discourse, to understand public judgment, to express national prejudices, to understand community concerns, to feel guilty — all these constitute the marks of social interplay and the platforms upon and between which conflicts are generated.

Harry's conflicts, however, are mostly with the "parole" — to continue with the Saussurean analogy — rather than with the "langue" of the system, with the manifestations of the rules rather than with the rules themselves. To the latter he, in fact, sticks to the ultimate consequences. He may be, in fact, quite accurately described as a "defender of the faith" whose major conflicts have to do with the protection of the system rather than with his personal attempts to question or change it. Thus, what Harry Angstrom insists upon whenever we identify his frustrations, pains, angers and the like, is not really a desire to change the rules of the game, but a compulsion to play the game better and to have others play it better too, according to existing rules. And this is where his little tragedies become more clearly manifest. Having placed absoluteness or essence in a world of relations, Harry's life becomes, temporarily at least, unbearable when the relations are altered, the rules changed, and the farce of absoluteness is exhibited. His very first escape from his wife on March 20, 1959, for example, was not a reaction against the rules of marriage, but against their being played out in such a fashion that only a second-rate life could be assured. As with his golf games, Harry can only keep his eyes on where the ball is supposed to go and gets angry and frustrated when he finds out that it actually went somewhere else. But the rules of the game are fixed for him: golf is golf, basketball is basketball, marriage is marriage, America is America. To change the rules which govern these worlds is to destabilize them, to change what he takes to be their very nature — something he is not about to allow to happen without resistance.

Having established this conservative posture of Harry, we understand better the reason why Updike, like a camera man in need of conflict, keeps changing the focus of his camera, forcing us in the process to perceive the decentration, the polyphony, that moves the wheel of the social text he portrays. In other words, Updike's Harry Angstrom is a man who, without understanding its constitutive elements or its syntax, "speaks" according to the "grammar" of the system. Thus, without a constantly changing environment, the essential ingredient of human life — tension — would be absent from the Rabbit trilogy. As Updike himself puts it, "to be a person is to be in a situation of tension, is to be in a dialectical situation. A truly adjusted person is not a person at all — just an animal with clothes on."[4] And Harry's tension, his feeling of disadjustment, has to do with and is generated by realizations which do not follow the system's basic grammar. Once in a while, no more than once every ten years, and then only for a few months, Harry is overrun by events and, to his distress, and sometimes to his relief, he is forced to adapt to new rules. Never acting as a ground-breaker or an avant-garde individual, a political activist or a captain of industry, which would obviously rob him of his middleness and averageness, Harry is always slow in readapting to new rules. By the time he accepts them, they have already been incorporated to the system as a whole. This explains the false impression one may get that Harry is questioning the establishment — a trap which has caught many critics — when in fact Harry, who before struggled to keep the engine of the system well-oiled and running as it always did, is now forced by circumstances to readapt to make himself again part of it. The state of tension, then, is a result of Harry's search for harmony within the social system and not an expression of his dynamism or revolutionary restlessness.

This conflict between permanence and change is at the heart of the Rabbit novels, and the selection and use of history serves fundamentally this very conflict. History's purpose is to generate actions capable of demonstrating how actual events can contribute to destabilizing the set of beliefs which have guided the protagonist's life. In a way which is perhaps visually more illustrative and helpful, we could say that the novels could be regarded as a set of widening concentric circles, having history as the first layer, followed by a layer of Harry's personal story, which faces more history, which generates more story, which faces more history, which generates more story, and so on indefinitely. This can easily be regarded as another "fraudulent outline" designed to avoid the "threat of infinite regress," as Levi-Strauss would put it, yet it helps us explain Updike's scenic concerns on the one hand, and the progression of the trilogy, which will become a tetralogy, on the other. Updike's elaborate consistency of agent and scene and the "overall coherence" of his "historical facts" is, as Hayden White says, "the coherence of the story [—a] coherence...achieved only by a tailoring of the "facts" to the requirements of the story form,"[5] but this consistency and coherence does not deny the scenic generative capacity, instead it only reveals the specific nature of human interaction with the scene. What Hayden White claims for the historical narrative, i.e., that "as a symbolic structure, the historical narrative does not reproduce the events it describes; it tells us in what direction to think about the events,"[6] is what I claim for the novels of the Rabbit trilogy and other novels with scenic preoccupations, e.g., Norman Mailer's *Armies of the Night*, Joseph Heller's *Good as Gold*, and Saul Bellow's *Mr. Sammler's Planet*, just to mention a few contemporary examples. Thus, the scene works as an intention, a finger pointing to segments of history and to segments of America which are believed to be, when put together, a recognizable picture of the impossible-to-grasp totality.

The story's more specific role, on the other hand, is to show how painful, pitiful, and sometimes, ludicrous the process of readaptation brought about by these events can be to a man who is but a worker, a simple man, somebody who occupies a space at the very center of the social and political spectrum. History and story will, thus, develop an active interplay throughout the three novels, one inviting the other. History will create action for the story, supplying the raw material for the artist to carve the image of his character and constructing plot, order, and control, by allowing itself to be placed within the borderlines of a limited universe; the story will require a selection of events which better serves the specific purposes of the self- perpetuating organism which it has become. The end result of this interplay is that at times history and story are so well blended together that it becomes difficult to clearly distinguish between them.

Another way of visualizing this integration is to consider a point of intersection located between two parallel vertical axes and two parallel horizontal axes. All these axes are in direct or indirect connection with each other, forcing to sprout between them a universe which is at one time limited and boundless, a location and an horizon, a fiction which the writer, the reader, and the characters cannot help connecting to the world of facts.

One vertical axis could stand for the historical activities, the events and circumstances in their actuality, as part of the public record, e. g., the Dalai Lama's escape from the Chinese forces; the meeting between Eisenhower and MacMillan, the Pope's visit, the Vietnam War, the oil crisis, the hostage crisis, etc.

The other vertical axis, running parallel but in opposite direction, so as to characterize their necessary indirect connection through the horizontal axes, is the axis of the activities of the characters, placed in time and space, and interacting with, through, and because of the surrounding events and circumstances, e. g., the Dalai Lama leading Rabbit to think of himself as a leader of a people; Apollo 11's journey to the moon making Rabbit think and verbalize his thoughts in terms of space imagery; the Pope's visit generating a heated and unpleasant discussion at Webb Murkett's home in *Rabbit is Rich*, etc.. Needless to say that the characters carry into the novels their own memories of past scenes, which invariably are used to evaluate the present, e.g., Rabbit, in *Rabbit, Run*, trying to recover the spirit of the winning team, expressed in his need to find a haven at his coach's place; Rabbit's recalling of the Ted Kennedy accident, ten years later, to help him explain and justify his helplessness at the fire scene in *Rabbit Redux*.

The third axis, running horizontally from left to right, is the reader's memory. He remembers not only the activities of the characters in each and every book, e.g., what Rabbit did early in the morning on March 22, 1959, what the name was of the cheesburger Jill and Harry had at the Burger Bliss in July 1969, etc., but also the memory of the local and national events and circumstances, the mood included, of those very same days. Here the reader, because of the precise scenic specifications, invariably helps to write the novel.

The fourth axis, running horizontally from right to left, and completing the intersection, is the author's vision and memory of the previous events in the earlier stories. Faced with new scenic conditions and the internal laws of probability, plausibility, coherence, and necessity, these events require a certain direction and force upon the author a certain preference on the axis of history. The particular closures of the open endings of the previous novels are somehow determined by the author's understanding of what would constitute acceptable behavior for his character under given conditions. When this behavior finds in the surrounding scene an event or circumstance which can broaden its meaning and significance, we are presented with wonderful imagistic parallels, e.g., Rabbit's middle age and the energy crisis; Rabbit's conflicts with his son Nelson in *Rabbit, Run* and *Rabbit Redux* and the hostage crisis which, in *Rabbit is Rich*, he views as kids plaguing the Carter Administration.

This conceptualization of the novels makes the forces of history, in their selection and transformation by the popular media — a fiction which Updike reselected and refictionalized — a conditio sine qua non for the novels' existence. It also makes the novels, at the same time, infinitely creative, since the stories' articulation perforce requires the social text in its constant state of mutability and conflict with the protagonist. Rabbit's expo-

sure to and reading of these conflicts, as well as his ways of
coping with them, is what the Rabbit trilogy is all about. And it
is through this exposure and through these conflicts that
Updike's America is revealed to us.

Updike's conception of the novels, then, it should be emphasized, has at its center — to use Kenneth Burke's terminology in
his *A Grammar of Motives* — more the "scene" than the "agent,"
"agency" or "purpose" of the human drama. It is precisely this
emphasis on the "scene" of the drama which allows us to perceive Updike's Harry as so, almost deterministically, moved by
the events and circumstances that surround his life. And it is
also this focus which makes us realize that the Rabbit trilogy is
not only a story of Harry but of all those who, like him, were
and are exposed to similar forces. Or, put differently, the trilogy,
because of the synechdochic mode in which it is cast, becomes
a story of middle America as much as it is Harry Angstrom's.
Harry and the scene, like man and the environment in the Marxist "grammar" of the world, are essential for action to occur, for
a story to exist, but Harry's chronic lack of control over his own
actions, his vague sense of purpose and direction, his clumsy
way of doing things (or should I say having things done to
him?) — all these suggest that the forces of scene, the forces of
history, are what ultimately makes Harry tick. Like a table lamp
which is fed by the positive and negative charges of the electric
system, Harry is fed by the forces of the establishment and by
those which oppose it. Like a movable multi-directional table
lamp, Harry also generates "light," but only to illuminate that
which "external circumstances" dictate.

My emphasis on these "external circumstances" is not an
attempt to transform the social text into the explicans of the
literary text, but rather to show how the moving back and forth
from Updike's text to the social text and back points to the scenic
origin of Updike's novels and how much the knowledge of these
scenic concerns can enrich our reading of his work. Thus, I argue
that the Rabbit trilogy, through its selective use of history, portrays a scene which (1) parallels the social, political, economic,
and cultural scene of the fifties, sixties and seventies; (2) acts

upon the characters as forces which generate actions, thoughts, judgments, and emotions; and (3) overruns Harry Angstrom's individuality, making him at times reflect and at other times refract the dominant forces of American society. Because he is moved more by forces of history rather than by his personal dreams or idiosyncrasies, Harry lives an essentially directed and teleguided life, being at different times, either victim or beneficiary, or both, of the social forces in conflict.

Only a scene-oriented approach, I believe, can account for the fundamental tensions in the Rabbit trilogy, for Harry Angstrom is much too static, anti-intellectual, and anti-problematic a character to be able to generate by himself significant conflicts. These are always primarily scene-centered and only then do we see them in their connection to the agent, purpose, and agency. Updike's need to place his novels so precisely in time and space expresses the conviction that his character, in his middleness, can only become unadapted and tensional if scene dislocations are promoted. Harry's conservative and adaptive tendencies would make him live in almost ape-like harmony with his environment had it not been made into a constantly changing element. Harry's purpose is not to change but to preserve what has been, unfairly he believes, changed, and his ways and means are those which the immediate scene supplies in its present state of ambiguity and confusion. These ways and means are as time-determined as the free-ways that surround him in the fifties, the offset machines that "outdate" him in the sixties, and the little gas-saving Toyotas that he sells in the seventies.

Thus, it is my conviction that an active scene (like Kenneth Burke I treat the characters in interaction also as scenic conditions or "environment" of one another)[7] on a fundamentally inactive character is what makes the Rabbit trilogy tick, and not the other way around, as many critics imply. This perception allows us to understand why Updike is almost maniacal in his concerns with time and space. In his latest book, *Roger's Version* (1986), for example, the action is not only precisely situated in time and space, but the combination of time and space becomes the very explanation for the origin of the universe. And Updike, a creator of universes himself, makes use of this combination, based on the latest scientific knowledge, to ridicule Dale's ludicrous attempt to prove God's existence with the use of computers and mathematical probabilities. Finally, the scenic approach also helps us to explain how, despite his directedness, middleness, and mediocrity, Harry manages to become a character who enjoys so much success with Updike's readers.

The scene-oriented approach, because it approximates the reader's perception of the text to the writer's creative process, also manages to bring into Updike's novels the realism of the social text, whose powerful polyphony it embodies. There is little doubt, as the following pages shall argue, that Updike wrote his Rabbit trilogy not only with a geographic map in front of him but also with a map of the socio-economic and political concerns of America in mind. Just as we can take a map and trace Rabbit's first journey from and to Reading on March 20, 1959, so can we trace most of Rabbit's social motions within the novels back to the corresponding social scenes outside of them. The shift of emphasis from agent to scene, because it makes such connections possible, enriches the reading and, thus, does justice to Updike's portrait of America. The following discussion of the pertinent criticism will illustrate more directly my use of Burke's terminology and the advantages of a scene-centered approach.

Notes

[1] John Updike, *Picked-Up Pieces* (New York: Fawcett Crest, 1966) 489.

[2] Kenneth Burke, *A Grammar of Motives* (Berkeley, Los Angeles, London: University of California Press, 1945) 201.

[3] Frederick Jameson, *The Prison-House of Language—A Critical Account of Structuralism and Russian Formalism* (Princeton: Princeton University Press, 1981) 35.

[4] John Updike, *Picked-Up Pieces* (New York: Fawcett Crest, 1966) 485.

[5] Hayden White, *Tropics of Discourse—Essays in Cultural Criticism* (Baltimore: John Hopkins University Press, 1978) 91.

[6] Ibid. 91.

[7] Kenneth Burke, Op. Cit. 7.

Chapter 1

From Agent To Scene

"Yet, so far as I can see, American history is normally absent from your work." "Not so; quite the contrary. In each of my novels, a precise year is given and a President reigns..."

(Picked-up Pieces).

The bulk of the criticism on Updike does not support or recommend a scene-oriented approach to his work. Almost all of the book-length works, in fact, if one applies Kenneth Burke's dramatist view of human actions, fall either under the category of idealism or mysticism, with only occasional inconsistent invasions of the spheres of scene and agency.

This is also true with the criticism on the Rabbit trilogy. Although most longer works were published in the seventies and, therefore, only include either the first or the first two books of the sequel, one can safely say that, had they written on the trilogy as a whole, very few of their earlier conclusions would have changed. Rachael C. Burchard, Edward Vargo, Joyce Markle, Suzanne Uphaus, and others give evidence enough that the scenic concerns of Updike in books like *Rabbit, Run* (1960), *The Centaur* (1963), and *Couples* (1968) have had little influence on their agent-centered interpretations, even though Updike referred to them, in an interview to Samuels as early as 1968, as being books directly related to a very specific time in American life, respectively, under the presidency of Eisenhower, Truman, and Kennedy. Another book, a book of criticism, *The Elements of John Updike* (1970), by Alice and Kenneth Hamilton, seemed to have a greater impact on their readings. The Hamiltons can be said to have set the tone of most of the critical work on Updike at least until 1980. *The Elements of John Updike* contains essentially an agent-centered approach whose idealism invariably leads to a mystification of scene, agency, and act. The Hamiltons' influence on the critics of the decade makes the discussion of their book necessary.

For obvious reasons, the Hamiltons discuss only the first book of the Rabbit trilogy. Although theirs is certainly among the richest books so far published on Updike's work, and although one may easily be led to agree with most of the support supplied for their arguments, sort of bewitched by the text's admirable clarity and fluency, one cannot help feeling somewhat cheated by the religious moralism which pervades the book. The implicit concern of the Hamiltons, in the hero-anti-hero line of reasoning, seems to be more to determine the blame rather than the causes of Harry's actions, with the visible intention to show how he failed to grasp those Heaven-sent messages, the divine grace, which could have saved him. Among those Heaven-sent messengers are the gas station attendant with whisky on his breath, his old coach Tothero, an old womanizer who also has whisky on his breath, the big Mouseketeer, and Eccles. Now, it is extremely difficult to argue about "the room of infinite possibilities," or about what could have happened had Harry told the gas attendant that he did not know exactly where he wanted to go, except that he had the south in his mind. Probably the course of events would have been different, though not necessarily his salvation. It would certainly have been different if Harry had reacted immediately to Tothero's first suggestion that he should return to Janice. If that would have meant his salvation is again extremely difficult to establish, for it implies a value-judgment involving the quality of life left behind and ever-controversial issues like the notion of marriage as a sacrament and the indissollubility of matrimony. Thus, although the Hamiltons chastize all those critics by whom "Rabbit has been judged...a saint indeed, a hero of the spirit challenging all adjustments to bourgeois society that bind the self to external standards at variance with the integrity of its inward vision,"[1] their way of looking at Rabbit is not very different. Besides being unable to identify the so-called "divine grace [which] is constantly moving behind the scenes,"[2] Rabbit is also seen as a romantic who is ignorant of the "patterns of actual existence"[3] and rejects "the healing that these could bring...not realizing that [his] dream of perfection can lead nowhere except to embracing death."[4]

The moralistic tone which is at the very base of the Hamilton's mental structure for one thing confuses divine grace with external circumstances, and, furthermore, obstructs the identification of causes which are at the level of scene rather than agent. This also explains why they cannot see Rabbit as a representative type of middle America, but only as an individual whose behavior is strictly anomalous and idiosyncratic, and whose salvation is possible only when placed at the realm of his individual acts, in the best style of the Christian tradition. I agree with Donald Greiner's comment that "Rabbit may be many things, but his heart is not always hard. What he does have is too many external circumstances beyond his control: school, family, work, and church all fail him."[5]

Implicit in the Hamilton's reasoning seems to be the idea that looking for causes beyond the realm of the strictly personal means to evade the question of responsibility, that is, by saying that the causes of Rabbit's actions are beyond Rabbit one would allow him to get away without paying the price for his deeds.

Edward Hallett Carr in his book *What is History* (1961) has, I believe, a clear and convincing answer to this concern when he points out that "cause and moral responsibility are different categories...since [moral responsibility] is a condition of social life [for] normal adult human beings."[6] One thing is to determine the responsibility of a person in a specific act, neglecting the individual's social interactions, quite another is to carefully look at the causes which led to that act in a specific social milieu and scenic circumstances, which only then can be thought of as causes with or without attenuating powers. What the Hamiltons style of study leads to is to too much judgment and too little study of causation, with the consequence that it condemns a man for social acts while removing the judgmental procedures from the social scene.

How does the Hamiltonian criticism of *Rabbit, Run* affect the reading of the novel? Their conception of Harry as a romantic hero, although not a revolutionary, makes him a totally inner-oriented protagonist, one who wants to transform the world according to his inner ideas of what it should be. As a consequence, Harry is blamed for not knowing well-enough the "actual existence" around him, or the reason why "his declension into the kingdom of death"[7] occurs. Although at least one of these points is perfectly defensible, the question which immediately comes to mind and which one must answer is "why did Rabbit run?" or "what did he run away from?" However varied the answers to these questions may be, they must necessarily include the following: (1) Harry disliked his family life (his wife, her cooking, her sloppiness, her drinking, her smoking, her TV-maniac behavior, her lack of understanding, her waning beauty, the lack of excitement, etc.); (2) he disliked his job as a gadget demonstrator and later as a used-car salesman; and (3) he disliked his present mediocre life and its deadness and nourished a dream of perfection reminiscent of his high school basketball days as a hero. All these answers, without making Rabbit into an automaton, are clearly of scenic nature and can be easily and earnestly supported by textual evidence. The Hamiltons themselves stumble into these answers all the time, but in their concern with the divine participation in human events they close their eyes to the social scene and instead fabricate a "theological" or mystical explanation which tells us that God is talking through the gas-attendant, through the big Mouseketeer, and through Tothero, telling Rabbit to go home to life and hope, but that unhappily Harry is just too dumb or too selfish to perceive it.

This has about the same implication as saying that history is a result of freak phenomena of nature, determined by a Godlike power, which we poor humans cannot understand and which are a vehicle through which God wants to tell us something. This order of explanation, however, belongs neither to criticism nor to common human behavior. As Edward Hallett Carr would say, nobody in his right mind would think of attributing the cause of a car accident which killed a man who was on his way to buy cigarettes at the shop on the corner to his smoking habits, especially when it is known that the driver of the car was drunk, driving recklessly, and did not stop at the red light. What the Hamiltons are doing amounts to almost the same thing, becoming a kind of interpretative perversity, asking us to see the accidental rather than the necessarily pertinent.

In the Hamiltons' view, then, two things seem to put Harry in motion: a divine force whose manifestations he cannot perceive in the surrounding scene, and his romantic search, a dream of success a la Willy Loman. Although he does share some of Willy Loman's romanticism, Harry hardly ever places his dream in a logical perspective, not even with a naive Dale Carnegie kind of simplistic clarity about rules for success. For Willy Loman the dream, right or wrong, is his way of life, a stubborn conscious refusal to accept·scenic entrapment, even if that means that he has to bargain with his life; in the character of Harry Angstrom, quite the opposite happens: the entrapment is sensed, an escape is attempted but is immediately frustrated, and entrapment ensues, demanding a new escape, which will again end in entrapment, making it clear that Harry's action is not determined by a dream but by spasm, instinct, a desire to feel adjusted to the scene as he once was and as Willy Loman has never been. His wish is there, no doubt, but it is a wish for readjustment rather than a wish to fulfill a personal dream. In this sense, Harry is more a retriever than a dreamer, more a goal keeper than a goal searcher. His emphasis on the learning of the rules of the game and playing it well also reflects Willy Loman's pragmatist's agency-centeredness aimed at beating the system at its own game. What is lacking in Rabbit is not Willy's determination or pragmatism but Willy's calculated purposiveness and Willy's capacity to mentally enact the steps and consequences of his acts. That is about as far as his dream goes. This is "the thing that wasn't there": a game well played. A demystification of the Hamiltons' gas attendant, Tothero, and the scene in general plunges Rabbit into a reality which can be better grasped by common mortals. This reality which affects Rabbit differently in the different decades generates in its movement more tensions than all of Harry's plans put together, for Harry in his motions has no plans, no purpose, no direction. He has principally what was. Little of what is and what will be truly

belongs to him, although, as with Willy Loman, it comes to him
"out of reality."[8]

Like the Magipeel peeler that Harry sells he too only touches
the surface of things, not realizing the broader changes that are
about to come or have already come. The Magipeel peeler is
itself not only an expression of a new type of national economy,
it also reveals that a new modern housewife has come to life,
one who is not necessarily a good cook, or a cleaning freak, but
one who will follow her male companion into the job market in
the years to come, imitating in the process also some of his
habits, good and bad. Had the Hamiltons perceived this play of
social forces, their comment that "even when he runs away,
grace is around him to warn him and guide him home,"[9] might
have been more generous towards the divine grace. The way it
is put, however, divine grace, if indeed it is there, can only send
Harry back to deadness. Only if death is taken as life, as in the
Christian paradox, can the environment Harry tried to leave
become its symbol. The application of the paradox to this specific
case, however, is unacceptable, telling us more about the critics
personal religious wishes and beliefs than about Updike's view
of American society during the fifties. This kind of criticism,
however, continues to influence critics more than a decade after
its publication. Almost every major book which has been written
on Updike's works follows a similar trend.

Rachael C. Burchard's *John Updike: Yea Sayings* (1971) also falls
into the same trap. Although she describes Harry as "an obedi-
ent child [who] listens to the 'authoritative' voice of modern
society,"[10] her reading concludes that Rabbit's search is "a search
for some kind of religious meaning...something Christianity
seems to have touched upon but which many who consider
themselves Christian have not recognized...it is the search of
that essence which impels us to search."[11]

This reading poses a few problems to start with. The "authoritative voice" identified by Burchard and to which Harry listens
is a recognition of scene-determined action, a scene which utilizes the socialized agency, television, to impose itself upon the
individual. But Burchard, following the Hamiltons' suggestion,

places a theologized scene behind the social scene as the ultimate determinant motive for Rabbit's action. This naturally hampers her understanding of the subtlety behind "the authoritative voice" which addresses Harry on television, blinding her to the fact that the voice is not as she believes an expression of the system's view in its positiveness, but a voice which stresses individuality within the acceptable boundaries of the authoritarian conformity which characterized the decade, as I demonstrate in the *Rabbit, Run* chapter of this book. Furthermore, Rabbit's decision to leave cannot be taken as a result of profound reflection on the meaning of the message of the Mouseketeers' words. In fact, Rabbit's decision to leave is essentially impulsive and anti-intellectual, characterizing more a spasm than a calculated and intelligent act, to which his constant leaving and returning attest. Finally, Burchard's view neglects the fact that, even in *Rabbit, Run*, which is the least topical of the novels, most of the things just happen to Rabbit, either because of an animal-like compulsion or because of a specific arrangement of circumstances.

Burchard's affirmation that "[Updike] as yet has not touched on racism or war, primary topics in contemporary fiction"[12] reflects more than her closeness to these issues (her book came out the same year *Rabbit Redux* was published, and she does not have it listed on her bibliography), it shows that her reading of *Rabbit, Run*, although it claims to see an individual victimized by his environment, assumes that the only fundamental social force operating in the novel is religion. This reductionistic reading explains why she did not perceive that *Rabbit, Run* is a novel of the fifties before it is a monologic novel about the "search for a religion to fit the needs of modern man."[13] The Hamiltons' powerful characterization of Rabbit as a hero engaged in a search, her historical proximity to *Rabbit, Run*, and her assumption that Updike had only written about himself in the previous novels — all this explains Burchard's lack of emphasis on the scenic nature of Updike's writings. Her expressed wish to see in 1971 an Updike who could write about his own time and place had already been granted, but she failed to see it.

Two years later, in 1973, two other book-length studies on Updike were published: Edward Vargo's *Rainstorms and Fire: Ritual in the Novels of John Updike* and Joyce Markle's *Fighters and Lovers: Theme in the Novels of John Updike*. Both are agent-centered studies profoundly influenced by the Hamiltons' Christian interpretation.

Our capacity to have many different reactions and feelings about the trilogy's protagonist in one single novel has led to endless debate on Harry's propensity to become at one time hero and villain. Although this should hardly be an issue, critics still find it puzzling to find a character who embodies these contradictory traits. Edward Vargo tries to point out the absurdity of this line of discussion. As he puts it, "the attempt to categorize Rabbit as a hero or anti-hero is, as the controversy suggests, a futile exercise. He is neither and he is both. Rabbit is basically an ambivalent middle-class American Christian living in a similarly ambivalent world. He is strong in potential but weak in action. He gains sympathy for his earnest desire for the something Beyond but gains contempt for his callous disregard of wife and children and Ruth."[14] As Vargo suggests, John Updike's portrayal of his character's ambivalence represents an attempt to move away from the manichean conception of life. It also attempts to shift the center of our interpretation from Harry, the agent, to an "ambivalent middle-class American Christian" scene. Vargo's attempt to contextualize Harry's ambivalence, however, does not succeed in ending the discussion of the hero-anti-hero controversy, for it does not manage to remove satisfactorily the focus of our attention from an agent who is "strong in potential but weak in action." His "earnest desire" and "callous disregard" are agent-centered attributes which a scene-centered approach would deemphasize in favor of a scene-agent and scene-purpose ratio. What Vargo's text shows, but hardly explores, is that a parallel world exists which is in consonance with, in harmony with, and as ambivalent as Harry, making him, therefore, an expression of his social milieu. What Vargo seems to have neglected in the specific case of *Rabbit, Run* is that Harry's search and his running away from wife, lover, and children constitute one only "act" — an "act" which is spasmodic and which, because it is what it is, negates its own validity and confirms Rabbit's superficial refusal of, and structural alliance with, the very things and people that anger him.

The hero-anti-hero controversy, then, for the Rabbit novels, is not only inappropriate — it is also misleading, for in its agent-centered perspective it fails to distinguish structural from surface conflicts, emotional spasms from meaningful actions. And it fails because the perspective somehow forces itself to attribute to Harry motives which he does not have or at least has not elaborated or refined — motives which are instead pressed upon him by unbearable present circumstances weighed against a pleasant and victorious past. In agent-centered approaches, however, Harry's directed life invariably becomes camouflaged, and what is essentially passive becomes active, with the implication that the motion toward accomodation becomes a heroic revolutionary quest. The gas attendant in *Rabbit, Run* does seem to have a point when he tells Rabbit that if you want to go somewhere you have to know where you are going. Direction, goal, purposiveness, control are what distinguishes action from spasm and motion.

Why Vargo tries to remove the agent-centeredness of his perspective and does not succeed can be explained by the broader conception of his work, a complicated exploration of pattern, myth, and celebration at the service of ritual — a combination of actions which he sees as Updike's way of reaching the transcendental. As we can see, the removal of the agent from the central perspective does not automatically mean a substitution of a socio-political scene. The ritualized, theologized scene is at the back of Vargo's thought, as it is behind everything the Hamiltons write. For Vargo, for example, Rabbit's home in the sixties was not set on fire by his neighbors or by real people — it was an act of God. Little wonder, then, that he visualizes and claims to see, behind Updike's scene, Updike's God — "a primitive, fierce, terrible God... the God of rainstorms and fire."[15]

Joyce Markle's book *Fighters and Lovers: Theme in the novel of John Updike* (1973) is a more sophisticated work and, although extremely agent-centered, it explores the scene-agent ratio more extensively than Vargo. Markle sees Rabbit in *Rabbit, Run* as a man who tries "to run clear of enmeshing social complexities. Cast into the imagery of basketball, the...novel sees Rabbit as a star player (a lover) who refuses to be forced into the role of team player, one who has no specialness. Rabbit's obsessive fear of becoming second rate, however, prevents his giving his gift of love to second-rate people without an underlying resentment and disgust. Thus, his ultimate response to social corporation is to reject it totally."[16]

This passage touches the most critical aspects of *Rabbit, Run*, those aspects which pose the greatest difficulty, especially because they are so easy to see and so difficult to interpret, constantly reminding us of Updike's comment that his fiction has a "yes, but" quality. The passage sees Rabbit as a runner who is trying to evade the "social complexities" which threaten him. Why do they threaten him? Because Rabbit, a man who had been a winner, a first-rate basketball player, finds himself, in the game of life, forced to play along with second-rate players. And, because he dislikes these players' refusal to improve their skills, he refuses to cooperate with them, and decides to flee.

The question which has to be raised, however, is how significant is Rabbit's decision to flee. Does it really mean his total rejection of social corporation? Are we not again exaggerating the significance of Rabbit's departures and forgetting the significance of his returns? Are we not forgetting what became of Rabbit only a few hours after his last run? Are we not forgetting that, although Harry seemed perfectly content with his pastoral idyll working for Mrs. Smith, he realizes that it is not a realistic enough occupation for a man who is a father and a husband? Doesn't Rabbit in fact abandon the pastoral idyll in order to return to "corporate" social life? Because we have to answer positively to these questions, the idea that Rabbit totally rejects "social corporation" becomes unacceptable, for it transforms him into an authentic and thoughtful rebel, which he is not. Rabbit is definitely more a lover than a fighter, and, although his love is for the first-rate, his fight is not against the structure of the team but against players who are not playing according to the rules of excellence which he believes can create a first-rate life. Thus, his flights are chronically aborted because they lack a clear sense of direction, and his fights are chronically lost, not because he is a spoiled egocentric child, but because the rules, more powerful, call him back whereas their realizations, more elusive but weaker, repel him. Rabbit has a rare glimpse of this distinction when, in *Rabbit Redux*, he remembers his indecision about Ruth after his return to Janice. When Janice expresses her disbelief that he had never tried to contact her, he answers simply, "I felt I shouldn't." Yet, the narrator tells us that "he sees now...that the rules were more complicated, that there were some rules by which he should have. There were rules beneath the surface rules that also mattered. She should have explained this when she took him back."[17] What the Rabbit of *Rabbit Redux* seems to have realized, ten years after his sexual adventures with Ruth, is that the rules which told him to return to Janice, the sacredness of marriage and fatherhood, are not in conflict with the responsibility for an act committed. Because he can no longer tell with the same clarity of the fifties which rules are central to his life, he has also doubts about what is right and what is wrong in the sixties. Like Janice in *Rabbit, Run*, he, too, in *Rabbit Redux*, has started to produce second-rate realizations of the rules.

Markle's book, however, offers some extremely good, although not uncontroversial, insights to *Rabbit Redux*. Independently taken, her chapter six is among the best studies on *Rabbit Redux* I have so far come across. Her analysis of the novel starts by taking a look at the major social forces in America in 1969, the year the action takes place. Having identified these forces, she dedicates a section of the chapter to each of them. The first force she discusses is White America—an America which is described as sterile, empty, dried up, cold, technologically-minded, and faithless. White America no longer trusts its leaders and its institutions, having broken even traditional historical myths like Washington and Lincoln by transforming them into "Disney-land Mechanical dummies."[18]

Opposed to this force is Skeeter's black militancy. Skeeter, Markle argues, is the lover and fighter of the novel, the one who can inspire, move, agitate the otherwise lethargic white establishment. The blacks as a race, because of their history of slavery and oppression, are the Americans who are not associated with the technological nightmare of the decade. Their association with liquids, Markle suggests, is also indicative of Updike's intention to oppose them to the dryness of white America. As in the boring baseball game to which Rabbit goes, life in America can find vitality in the sixties especially in blacks, even when it means to threaten them, to chase them, or to kill them.

Markle also dedicates a section of her book to the discussion of the Vietnam War, demonstrating how inter-related this issue and the black issue are. Because Skeeter, who fought in the war, can so vividly describe its horrors, he in a way manages to bring the war to America with him. And Markle also does an excellent job of showing how Skeeter uses his war experience to evaluate present-day America. His revolutionary view, which preaches the destruction of the system, is also a theology, a belief that God is manifesting himself through the horrors of war in order to ultimately show man's folly and the need to unify the races. And Skeeter sees himself as the black Jesus who will come to redeem America.

Markle's idea that the self-centered lover of the previous novel has now become Skeeter is, however, contrived and farfetched. It serves very well the thesis of her book, but it does not contribute to the understanding of Rabbit's trajectory. Markle's need to find a character who is above all religious, someone who, because of it, yields spiritual energy and vitality to America, forces her into the world of Skeeter as if it were a natural development of what Harry had been ten years earlier. As with Phillip Vaughn's argument, Markle does not see the Harry of *Rabbit Redux* as a continuation of the Harry of *Rabbit, Run*. Instead, here Skeeter has become the new Harry, and the old Harry has died out or dried up. This interpretation, it must be said, neglects a few quite crucial aspects of the novel. For one thing, it forgets the elementary idea that the second book of the trilogy keeps up the story of Rabbit, with or without the same energy of the fifties; It also forgets that the very title of the second book proposes a reconsideration of the character discussed in the first novel; and, finally, the revolutionary Skeeter, whose presence in the book is really limited to one of its four sections, has very little to do with the Rabbit of the first novel, if religiosity is for one brief moment put aside. It is indeed curious to see that Markle is able to jump from one extreme of the ideological spectrum to the other with such ease. Why can we not, for example, identify the Rabbit energies of the fifties with the hippies, the counterculture and its mysticism? Why not with Stavros or Mim? These are milder, less radical views of social reform which are much more suitable to the spasms of the Harry of the fifties. It becomes a blatant violation of all logical expectations that precisely he who preaches the destruction of the system should be considered a natural development of the Harry of *Rabbit, Run*, when the Harry of that novel proves to be so enmeshed in the system that his trajectory is one of indecision, lack of direction, and confusion — so unlike Skeeter in all respects, except for the one aspect which Markle elected to be the most important, i.e., that both claim to be Christ-like figures, self-appointed saviors, and mystics. Although this may be so — one can never be positive as to how seriously one is supposed to take these religious claims — the two novels cannot be read together with Markle's frame of mind without seriously distorting Rabbit's story, and, along with it, the story of white America, and, especially, the story of black America that it contains. Markle's chapter on *Rabbit Redux* is, in isolation, quite convincing, but, as part of her larger argument, it is indefensible. It reveals a regrettable lack of understanding of the ideological spectrum which Updike so carefully portrays. As I point out in the *Rabbit Redux* chapter of this book, Skeeter, Jill, Stavros, Rabbit, Mr. Angstrom, and Mr. Springer — each of these characters stand for a different color of the ideological spectrum. Skeeter is obviously at a considerable distance to the left of Jill, and even farther away from the liberal Stavros or the conservative Democrats and Republicans, here represented by Harry's father and his father-in-law. Markle's analysis, brilliant as it otherwise is, misses this fundamental ideological picture.

R. A. Regan's article "Updike's Symbol of the Center" (1974), is a Jungian reading of Updike's *Assorted Prose*. Regan moves away from fire, fighters, and lovers, to argue that the center of Updike's universe is the "I" or "eye." His argument is centered around this passage from the "First Person Singular" chapter of *Assorted Prose*:

> My geography went like this: in the center of the world lay our neighborhood of Shillington, and around that, Berks County. Around Berks County there was the State of Pennsylvania, the best, the least eccentric, state in the Union. Around Pennsylvania, there was the United States, with a greater weight of people on the right and a greater weight of land on the left. For clear geometrical reasons, not all children could be born, like me, at the center of the nation. But that some children chose to be born in other countries seemed sad and fantastic. There was only one possible nation: mine. Above this vast rectangular, slightly (the schoolteachers insisted) curved field of the blessed, there was the sky, and the flag, and mixed up with both, Roosevelt.[19]

The passage clearly places the young boy at the center of the world, the same way Joyce had Stephen Dedalus think of himself in *The Portrait of the Artist as a Young Man*. But Updike's young man, not unlike Joyce's, has an acute awareness that he is placed in a very specific place (Shillington) and in a very specific time (Roosevelt). And he also has an obvious sense of belonging, a "sense of place" — a sense which translates into a middleness which generates pride, for it makes the place not only the least "excentric" but also the "best" in the nation. That Updike chose to distinguish between childhood and boyhood in the "First Person Singular," after having chosen "boyhood" as part of the chapter's title, shows how careful one has to be when reading him. "Our childhood," says Updike, "is what we alone have had; our boyhood is what any boy in our environment would have had."[20] The attempt to commonize the young boy's experience, the need to regard him as someone placed at the "center" of the nation and between events central to the nation (The Great Depression and World War II) — these are attempts to find middleness, representativeness, that which the particular scene of Pennsylvania has in common with America as a whole. It is easy to see how this applies directly to the methodology employed in the creation of the Rabbit Novels. Thus, the "I" Regan sees is there, no doubt, as a sort of Jungian collective unconscious. Updike pluralized the first person singular the moment he started giving titles to the subsections of his chapter. Titles like "A Boyhood," "History," "Geography," "Democrats," "Now," "Environment," "Schools," "The Playground," "The Movie House," and others are so scenic that one cannot fail to see the "I" being diluted in the collective. Yet, Updike's collective "I" is also historicized and contextualized — it is not a universal archetype. Updike's "I" is not only plural — it is also time and place-specific. It is historically produced.

Regan's I-centered reading, then, fails to see the interference of a historicized scene. This is especially meaningful when one takes the Rabbit trilogy into account. Rabbit, for instance, loses his way because the freeway-highway system operates as an enslaving web, and he finds it impossible to escape; the television system invades his home, makes his wife into a videomaniac and forces him into silence. In the sixties, his wife decides, as a woman looking for her liberation, to join the labor market and have her own sexual adventures, and Harry finds himself stuck, along with America, with the Vietnam war, the hippie movement, the black civil rights movement, the urban riots, and the draft resisters, having to face them, regardless of his willingness to do so; finally, here, too, in the seventies, Harry is carried by the events of the energy crisis and the Toyota invasion — so carried in fact that in the specific "scene" he works, his "Toyota agency," the action of selling his cars is performed by the events rather than by the salesman, so much so that Harry at times feels useless at the lot and his friend and employee, Charlie Stavros, complains that the times of real selling are over. Now, little personal quality or merits are needed, for the force of events is such that "the cars sell themselves," and Rabbit, because of it, finds himself rich. These are some of the forces at work in the three novels, and they are forces which, because they are "scene-centered" rather than "agent-centered," run head-on against the very base of Regan's generalization. As Donald J. Greiner puts it in his *John Updike's Novels*: "Rabbit reacts to every stimulus, every emotion....In this sense he is an extreme product of the placid, hermetic Eisenhower years, a kind of historical artifact."[21] The merit of Regan's article lies, I believe, in his attempt to pluralize the agent. Updike's study on Whitman's "egotheology," (1977) confirms Regan's perspective. Whitman's "Song of Myself," Updike argues, would have been a tribute to egotism and even selfishness were it not for its all-embracing scenic absorbtion which forces the "I" into plurality. But the plurality of Updike's "I" does not mean universality. Instead, it is an abstraction of the marks of time and space on man and vice-versa. Regan's interpretation, despite its attempt to collectivize the agent, remains blind to the scenic.

In 1980 Suzanne Henning Uphaus made an attempt to reconcile the theologized or mystic scene of the Hamiltons and Edward Vargo with the more worldly socio-political scene which, after *Couples* (1968), *Bech: a Book* (1970), *Rabbit Redux* (1971), and *The Coup* (1978) became impossible to deny. To bring these worlds together, Uphaus wrote a wonderful little book with the unpretentious title *John Updike* (1980). Uphaus's main argument is that "all Updike's work [presents] these two worlds, the natural and the supernatural, [which] are present either implicitly or implied...and are basic to an understanding of it."[22] Thus, she argues, "Updike sees man as a dichotomous creature, split between his physical desires on the one hand and his spiritual yearnings on the other...in all the novels except *A Month of Sundays* the natural and the supernatural, the physical and the spiritual dimensions of man, stay stubbornly apart. They fail to integrate."[23] What this means to the interpretation of the Rabbit trilogy (Uphaus, obviously, only discusses *Rabbit, Run* and *Rabbit Redux*) is that Harry is a man split in two, a man who does not know if he should pledge allegiance to the physical world, the material world which surrounds him and the physical compulsions within him, or if he should pursue the supernatural, i.e, Christ, God. The uncertainty which Harry faces is what would explain his sequence of departures and returns. And because, society no longer offers the possibility of blending traditional religion with contemporary life, Harry must escape. But, because escape is impossible, Uphaus argues, "the contemporary human condition is reinforced [and] the final lesson is perhaps one of compromise with the world as it is."[24] Again, the hero-anti-hero approach places the action heavily in Harry's hands, as if his intellectual and spiritual manifestations were a long cultivated attribute and his actions a result of his rational decisions to give his life some meaning. As we have seen, they are not. Because Uphaus views the novel with a hero-anti-hero frame of mind, she claims that "our traditional conception of the heroic action, [which] does not involve running away"[25] tends to condemn Rabbit, but that his "spiritual drive, his unwillingness to compromise"[26] and his capacity to resist against a world of " corroding hypocrisy"[27] make him heroic once more. Her approach not only transforms Harry into a revolutionary questioning the very structure of his social system but also proves to be embarrassing when we learn what happens to Harry only hours after his last "escape" in *Rabbit, Run*. The straw-fire of his angry last departure burns out just as fast as his first attempt to escape is aborted. Hardly a revolutionary, hardly heroic, Harry is in search of adaptation rather than change. His conservative nature, however, becomes more patently clear in *Rabbit Redux*.

Uphaus's reading of *Rabbit Redux* is in a strange way even more agent-centered. "Updike's characters become the agents of history,"[28] she claims quite accurately after a discussion of the major social forces — blacks, hippies, and Vietnam — which she describes as being "not only the background for the novel...but the basis for its action."[29] Having apparently forgotten her earlier chapter, Uphaus now claims that "it could be argued that *Rabbit Redux* is Updike's greatest achievement, for it is written without reference to the Christian or classical myths upon which his earlier works depended. Rabbit reflects this secularization in his lack of spiritual drive and his consequent loss of that tension

between the spiritual and the carnal that most of Updike's pro-
tagonists struggle with."[30] What Uphaus could and should have
added is that the events of the sixties are precisely the fuel which
moves the locomotive of the train of history, a train which Harry
is forced to ride regardless of his willingness, and which Skeeter
and Jill also ride, but not as passengers, as fuel. They are events,
they are scene, whereas Harry, passion rather than action, travels in the caboose. Jill, the hippie, offers herself to Harry. He
takes her with him when he leaves Buchanan's party because
she wants him to and because "they want [him] to,"[31] not
because it was his idea. Similarly, the black militant, Skeeter,
does not wait for Harry's invitation; instead, Harry comes home
from work one evening and finds him there, forcing Harry to
react accordingly. In other words, Harry is overrun by the events
and forced to adapt, which he does with difficulty. But Harry
anticipates nothing and predicts nothing. As Jill puts it, with
little exaggeration, "[his] life has no reflective content; it's all
instinct."[32] Thus, to confuse Harry with an "agent of history" is
to see a wild-roaring lion where only a sheep patiently grazes.
Uphaus does not perceive that Harry stands as a symbol of middle America, an America caught in-between the forces that make
history— the dominant economic and political powers and the
progressive forces which demand change. Harry is caught in-
between, forced to helplessly watch the fire burn down his
house while the instituted force of the establishment declares
the hippie dead, the Negro a dangerous arsonist, and him one
of America's "solid citizens."[33] No wonder, then, that standing
over the rubble of his destroyed house, Harry hallucinates. In
his hallucination he sees the past and the future, that which has
died—his daughter Becky, "the freshening sky above Mount
Judge"[34]—and that which is to come—"a sullen sky…the color
of a storm sky,"[35] his son Nelson. "And he is the man in the
middle,"[36] pressed between life and death, past and future, an
object of the cosmos, an object of history.

A book which, at first sight, suggests some similarities with
my scene-oriented approach is Philip H. Vaughan's *John Updike's
Images of America* (1981). His book opens with the powerful dec-

laration of belief that "John Updike—more than any other contemporary American novelist—explores the many paradoxes, complexities, and mysteries to be found in our society....Updike—as well as certain other novelists— provides a greater interpretive framework than do historians, sociologists, psychologists, or other social scientists for the understanding of such real human problems as loneliness, isolation, aging, and morality."[37] His book, however, never lives up to this thesis and becomes little more than plot summaries, without a conclusion or an attempt to show how or in what ways, for instance, Updike's interpretive framework is "greater" than that of historians or sociologists. Thus, despite the promise and the mostly good plot summaries, the book adds very little to the understanding of the meaning of the historic in the fictional. Indeed, the book would be a total disappointment were it not for its sporadic insights which, without much support and without references or notes, manage to convey to the reader a sense that Updike's concern is, above all, social and national rather than individual and personal. Nonetheless, although this perspective allows him, for instance, to say that *Rabbit, Run* "leaves us with a feeling that Updike sees through the comatose tranquility of modern suburbia and envisions a future torn by social disorder,"[38] he jumps to the false conclusion that "Harry Angstrom represents in fictional form one of the many different types of protest that reached a climax in the 1960s."[39] This frontally contradicts everything Harry came to stand for immediately after his three-month adventure in *Rabbit, Run* and cannot be taken seriously. Furthermore, it would be extremely difficult to trace a straight line to any character in *Rabbit Redux,* except to Harry himself, especially because the major forms of protest in the sixties came from blacks, minorities, women, students, and intellectuals. Middle America, where Harry found his niche, continues to be middle America, "the silent majority" of the sixties. Although the wheel of history may seem to be turning faster, Harry, at its center is in no danger of falling out. Thus, to establish a direct connection between Harry and Skeeter (the black protest), Harry and Jill (the hippie counterculture), Harry and Stavros (minorities), Harry and Janice or Mim (women), or any other rebellious or revolutionary force of the sixties, is to see in the "domestic Rabbit" of *Rabbit, Run* a force which he does not have, while neglecting the more powerful scene-generated forces of guilt, duty, and group or team responsibility, the essential grammar which he shares with middle America. That we actually find Harry in the sixties living in a house so much like the other houses in the vicinity, and that we see him defined to us, and acting, as a "solid citizen" or as part of the "silent majority" should not come to us as a surprise. It is merely an indication that the institutional forces had a greater control over, and appeal to him than critics tend to see.

Our interest in Vaughn's view, it must be said, lies less in the solidity and coherence of his argument than in the significance it has for the Updike criticism in the making—a criticism which a decade after the Hamiltons' influential book is gradually discovering the importance of scene. Vaughn's book is an interesting reminder that a change of focus is under way.

Another major step in the direction of an Updike criticism which does not nourish the old refusal to see his concern with placing his work in time and space was taken by Kathleen Lathrop in 1982. Kathleen Lathrop's still unpublished dissertation is titled *Updike on America: The Expanding Vision of John Updike in his Post-Olinger Novels* (1982). Lathrop's work, to which mine is significantly indebted, is the first meaningful attempt to study Updike's novels with a more scene-oriented approach in mind. Our disagreements have more to do with our different ways of perceiving the dynamism of the social forces at work and, consequently, our different strategies of organizing these forces for the purpose of argumentation. Lathrop's thesis is primarily an attempt to deny charges made by many critics that Updike's work is "too heavily reliant on autobiography and limited by an outdated realistic mode."[40] Her study of the post-Olinger novels shows very convincingly that, not only has Updike gone beyond the autobiographical but that more and more he shows a concern with the political and social awareness of his work and with "a formal inventiveness often overlooked by his critics."[41]

As we can see, Lathrop's argument is an answer to Rachael C. Burchard's contention in the early seventies that Updike's writing had note yet touched major national social issues and was far too dependent on his personal experience. Although she agrees with Burchard when it comes to the reading of the Olinger novels, Lathrop points to Updike's "expanding vision" — a vision deeply rooted in the social forces — in the later novels. My understanding is that even in the earlier novels the scenic concerns are heavily present and that they are there as essential as they are to his Rabbit trilogy and other later novels. Lathrop's work is, however, despite its still largely agent-centered reading of *Rabbit, Run* — which she claims "can...be read both as a personal quest novel and as a criticism of American life at mid-century"[42] — the most outspoken expression of the need to see the social and scenic dimension of Updike's work. Lathrop's is the first book-length study to include all three of the Rabbit novels. Two years later, Robert Detweiler and Donald Greiner added two new books to this list.

Robert Detweiler's book *John Updike* (1984), in less than two hundred pages, discusses almost all of Updike's prose, including the three Rabbit novels. Like Lathrop and unlike Joyce Markle, he sees the last two Rabbits as a continuation of the first. He sees Rabbit as evolving "from an irresponsible and romantic drifter to lower-middle-class conservative and patriot [having in *Rabbit is Rich*] pushed through to a bit more humanity."[43]

Rabbit, Run is seen as a quest novel in which a non-hero, not an anti-hero, searches for "a vanished grail."[44] Rabbit's quest is, thus, futile, for he himself cannot define what he is looking for, wandering aimlessly, moved more by compulsion than by a goal. "He is not," Detweiler tells us, "a radical individualist asserting his total freedom as he challenges the mores of his society. Nor is he an ultimately lovable and forgivable picaresque rascal who disguises a stellar nature behind the scrapes that involve him. The antihero has qualities that society may not

value, but they are at least of the kind that give him individuality
and identity and that provoke an unwilling admiration. Irresponsible, undependable, and gutless, Rabbit is the quintess-
ence of the nonhero."[45]

What replaces the vanished grail this non-hero is looking for?
In *Rabbit, Run* it is the glory and adulation of his heroic basketball
days and the sexual act. After having replaced the holy grail
with his past physical prowess and sexuality, Rabbit has to
become stationary, nostalgically looking at himself, ending
where he began, and being, finally, victimized by the tragedy of
not learning.

It is at this point in the discussion that Detweiler's criticism
acquires an exclusive psychoanalytical orientation. He argues
essentially that Rabbit's present drives are oedipal in nature and
that his search is really for a woman who is both a whore and a
mother at the same time—Ruth being precisely the type he
needed, but that "he is much too entangled in the knots of his
personality, too vacillating in his capricious sense of obligation,
to carry through a divorce and a remarriage. Instead he does—
typically— nothing; and he loses Ruth."[46] He is, thus, "an
abnormal figure"[47] victimized by his oedipus-oriented relation
to women, by "the revenge of eros."[48]

Unhappily, Detweiler does not continue with this kind of analysis when he comes to the discussion of *Rabbit Redux*. Instead,
he approaches the novel in terms of its social representativeness,
its "orchestration of tropes,"[49] its "instructive motion"[50] and its
"fictive risks,"[51] frustrating one's natural expectation of a consistent approach to all three Rabbit novels. Detweiler still sees Rabbit as a creature without control over his life, living an essentially
"glandular existence," but here Rabbit is no longer seen as being
maneuvered by his oedipus complex. Here he is pushed around
by the forces of history, transformed by them, led to "an increasing political awareness"[52] and forced by the power of events to
"drift to the left."[53]

In *Rabbit is Rich* Detweiler sees a similar national concern in
motion. Rabbit again becomes an expression of the environment, jogging like his president and becoming rich because of

the specific arrangement of the national and international economic forces. Surprisingly, Detweiler pays little attention to the complex father-son relationships, to Harry's search for Ruth, concentrating especially on the sexual adventures of the couples in the novel. Here Detweiler seems more concerned with showing that Updike is not a pornographic writer as some claim but that the sexual explicitness has the intention to embody the triviality and emptiness of the characters' life.

Detweiler's study of the trilogy is especially good in demonstrating the lack of control Rabbit has over his life. Even his discussion of *Rabbit, Run* shows that Rabbit is at the mercy of forces which he cannot control, including psychological ones. Clearly, however, Detweiler's interpretation and mine go in different directions, i.e. he claims that Rabbit, as an abnormal human being, distorts his social relations, especially with the opposite sex, without understanding why he acts the way he does. My interpretation of *Rabbit, Run*, although it does not deny the presence of these Oedipal forces, emphasizes Rabbit's representativeness as a Middle American Radical, a quite "normal" one in fact, who can no longer bear the contradictions between a life which he believes is possible to be lived, because it WAS lived, and the life which he in actuality has to live. And, because Rabbit can be taken as a "normal" middle American who believes in marriage, fidelity, sacredness of authority, institutions, and achievements, his attempt to recapture the lost glory of the past can very well be read as a loss of the victorious common-purposeness of the America of the World War II days and the years immediately following, as Leo Braudy suggests in *The Harvard Guide to Contemporary American Writing* (1979),[54] an America which at the end of the fifties was beginning to show the first signs of internal division.

Similarly, if Detweiler's reasoning is pursued, Rabbit's relation to Eccles has to be taken as a relation of an abnormal individual with another one who is also abnormal and loaded with good intentions. Yet, Eccles is vested with the authority of the church, an authority which, like Soupy in *Rabbit is Rich*, and the aborted Eccles of early manuscripts of *Rabbit Redux*, may seem awkward and even ludicrous at times, but which, nonetheless, is there and is part of the Springers' and Angstroms' lives. Furthermore, Eccles stands for a very significant trend in the American church of the fifties, the secularized church, a church which, unlike Kruppenbach and his pietist attitudes, preaches direct involvement with the human worries of the Rabbits of this world. Detweiler's criticism, by assuming that Harry and Eccles are abnormal, not only removes Harry's middleness and representativeness, but fails to explain Harry's attempt to recover the victorious spirit of the first-rate team, which is central to the novel. Tothero's presence throughout the book, along with the basketball imagery, and Eccles's presence are not accidental; they are structural and stand respectively for the post-war successful America and the evaluations of that success in terms of particular realizations in the daily game of life. When seen in this light it is truly remarkable to see how Tothero, Eccles, and Harry agree in their concern to keep the old rules alive. Marriage, even a bad marriage, has to be maintained. The rules are sacred, despite our sporadic vacillations and poor performances. As with the golf game Harry plays with Eccles, one has to keep at it, trying and trying and trying again, until a better performance, perfection perhaps, is possible. All this conflict is absent from Detweiler's interpretation. And considering the date of publication of his book, it represents, as a whole, a reversal in the trend towards scene-oriented studies. It is too early to determine if his book is the beginning of a new psychoanalytic trend. Donald Greiner's book seems to suggest that it is not.

Greiner's book *John Updike's Novels* (1984) has a chapter on the Rabbit trilogy entitled "Why Rabbit Should Keep on Running?" His answer is a long and detailed one, but it can be summarized in one sentence: Rabbit should keep on running in order to stay alive and keep up the fight against the forces that oppress him. The assumption is that an escape is possible staying within the system. Thus, the openendedness of the individual novels is emphasized, although the novels are analyzed as a sequence. The running of *Rabbit, Run* is, thus, equivalent to the journey to the motel at the end of *Rabbit Redux* and to the trip to the Caribbean and to the move to the new house at the end of *Rabbit is Rich*. Each of these final moves is seen as a step towards freedom. It is easy to perceive that Greiner's view and Rabbit's are very close and that neither seems to perceive the entrapment that will follow. This is especially true with Greiner's reading of the last two of the Rabbit novels. Greiner claims that Harry is finally a more mature man for at least he "can define roughly what he wants...the years and the pounds and the comfort of money have combined to readjust his sights closer to earth: A home of his own, a life without Nelson, a real live daughter, and one hour in bed with confident Cindy."[55] Ironically, when we just for one moment think of what Rabbit wanted in the fifties, we cannot help seeing how little he has changed. Greiner, in refusing to see the previous entrapments which followed the last scenes of the previous novels, also fails to see that Rabbit in *Rabbit is Rich*, in his new home, has just placed himself in a dead end street. Greiner's final portrayal of Rabbit as a member of the "honor roll of American culture"[56] because "he believes in the possibility of new territories, the glow of affirmation, and the renewal of love"[57] is a pompous misrepresentation. The sentence, however, becomes somehow representative of this unevenly written book, whose wonderful insights are sadly counterbalanced by unacceptable recontextualizations of Updike's text for obvious argumentative purposes, and by judgments and inferences which frequently find no support unless through textual contrivance. Thus, sentences like "[Harry] is comfortable enough in *Rabbit is Rich* to put the headlines behind him"[58], and "is not so tied to the news of the day as in *Rabbit Redux*[59], or "*Rabbit Redux* is the novel in which Harry Angstrom finally says good-bye to his past"[60] or, still, "it is not that Rabbit is a racist, but that he distrusts mobility by those who do not accept the system"[61], these sentences find no support in my reading of Updike's text, and my discussion of the novels will show why this is so.

These are the major book-length critical works so far produced on Updike's fiction. A flood of short articles has been produced (some of them were compiled and published in book form, e.g.

David Thorburn and Howard Eiland's *John Updike — A Collection of Critical Essays*, and William R. Macnaughton's *Critical Essays on John Updike*) and published in major and minor journals, magazines, and newspapers throughout the country. Because these articles are mostly studies of very specific aspects of specific works, I shall discuss their applicability or not to my thesis only when they are directly pertinent and clearly enrich the discussion in the following chapters.

It should be said, however, that criticism on Updike has so far failed to produce or apply an approach which can explain the Rabbit trilogy without having to shift from theology to psychology to sociology and back, according to the critics' thetic needs, and without having to force upon the text, almost perversely, interpretations of incidents which are frequently more an exercise in mysticism than an exercise in criticism and logic. As we have seen, a long distance has been traveled since the Hamiltons' influential book. Most of the time, however, the journeys had a very similar point of departure and a very similar destination, so that although a lot was added in mileage little was added to the original scenery. With the publication of *Rabbit Redux* (1971) some changes started to occur, but it was not easy to replace the Hamiltonian notions. Only after *The Coup* (1978) was published did we start to get some, still very timid, scene-oriented interpretations. These interpretations started to suggest new possibilities for the reading of Updike's work, possibilities which I decided to explore and to apply consistently to the Rabbit trilogy.

Notes

[1] Alice and Kenneth Hamilton, *The Elements of John Updike* (Grand Rapids, Michigan: Williams B. Eerdmans Publishing Company, 1970) 142.

[2] Ibid. p. 17.

[3] Ibid. p. 142.

[4] Ibid. p. 142.

[5] Donald Greiner, *John Updike's Novels* (Athens, Ohio: Ohio University Press) 52.

[6] Edward Hallet Carr, *What is History?* (New York: Vintage, 1961) 124.

[7] Alice and Kenneth Hamilton, *The Elements of John Updike* (Grand Rapids, Mich.: Williams B. Eerdmans Publishing Company, 1970) 153.

[8] Arthur Miller, *Death of a Salesman* (Harmondsworth: Penguin, ed. 1984) 12.

[9] Ibid. p. 146.

[10] Rachael Burchard, *John Updike: Yea Sayings* (Carbondale and Edwardsville: Southern Illinois University Press, 1971) 44.

[11] Ibid. p. 44.

[12]Ibid. p. 4.

[13] Ibid. p. 5.

[14] Edward Vargo, *Rainstorms and Fire: Ritual in the Novels of John Updike* (Port Washington, New York: Kennikat Press, 1973) 73.

[15] Ibid. p. 84.

[16] Joyce Markle, *Fighters and Lovers: Theme in the Novels of John Updike* (New York: New York University Press, 1979) 3.

[17] John Updike, *Rabbit Redux* (New York: Fawcett Crest, 1971) 66.

[18] Joyce Markle, Op. Cit. p. 153.

[19] John Updike, *Assorted Prose* (New York: Alfred Knopf, Inc., 1979) 163.

[20] Ibid. p. 165.

[21] Donald Greiner, *John Updike's Novels* (Athens, Ohio: Ohio University Press, 1984) 50.

[22] Suzanne Henning Uphaus, *John Updike* (New York: Frederick Ungar Publishing Co., 1980) 5.

[23] Ibid. p. 6.

[24] Ibid. p. 25.

[26] Ibid. p. 22.

[27] Ibid. p. 23.

[28] Ibid. p. 90.

[29] Ibid. p. 80.

[30] Ibid. p. 76.

[31] John Updike, *Rabbit Redux* (New York: Fawcett Crest, 1971) 122.

[32] Ibid. p. 202.

[33] Ibid. p. 286.

[34] John Updike, *Rabbit, Run* (New York: Fawcett Crest, 1960) 286.

[35] Ibid. p. 287.

[36] Ibid. p. 287.

[37] Philip Vaughn, *John Updike's Image of America* (Reseda, Ca.: Mojave Books, 1981) v.

[38] Ibid. p. 20.

[39] Ibid. p. 20.

[40] Kathleen Lathrop, "*Updike on America: The Expanding Vision of John Updike in his Post-Olinger Novels*," diss., New York State University, 1984, iv.

[41] Ibid. p. iv.

[42] Ibid. p. 23.

[43] Robert Detweiler, *John Updike.* (New York: Twayne Publishers, Inc., 1972) 178.

[44] Ibid. p. 33.

[45] Ibid. p. 38.

[46] Ibid. p. 42.

[47] Ibid. p. 43.
[48] Ibid. p. 43.
[49] Ibid. p. 127.
[50] Ibid. p. 131.
[51] Ibid. p. 134.
[52] Ibid. p. 132.
[53] Ibid. p. 133.
[54] Leo Braudy, In Daniel Hoffman, ed., *The Harvard Guide to Contemporary American Writing*. (Cambridge and London: Harvard University Press, 1979) 86.
[55] Donald Greiner, *John Updike's Novels* (Athens, Ohio: Ohio University Press, 1984) 92.
[56] Ibid. p. 98.
[57] Ibid. p. 99.
[58] Ibid. p. 86.
[59] Ibid. p. 85.
[60] Ibid. p. 80.
[61] Ibid. p. 70.

Chapter 2

The Domestic Rabbit

"You are born into one political contract or
another, whose terms, though they sit very lightly
at first, eventually, in the form of the draft, or taxes,
begin to make very heavy demands on you. The
general social contract—living with other people
driving cars on highways—all this is difficult, it's
painful. It's a kind of agony really"
(Picked-up Pieces).

Harry Angstrom, in *Rabbit, Run*, lives in Mount Judge, a suburb
of Brewer (Reading), Pennsylvania. It is from there that he
departs on March 20, 1959, a Friday evening, and stays away
until the third week of June of the same year. He stays during
this time with Ruth, a prostitute who is introduced to him by his
former basketball coach, Tothero.

Harry had driven the whole night away from Brewer, only to
discover that, lost in a maze of freeways and secondary roads,
he had returned to his point of departure. Back in Brewer, he
decides to look for Tothero, who immediately, but not very
emphatically, tells him that he should go back to his wife and
try a reconciliation. At the end of the day, however, Tothero
decides that what Harry (Rabbit) really needs before returning
home is some adventure, as if he knew that this adventure with
other women would invariably send him back to his wife, Janice.
This go-return pattern will prove to be characteristic of all of
Rabbit's future departures.

That we can be so sure about the precise date of Rabbit's first
flight from home reveals Updike's concern with historically situating the events narrated in his novel. From the very beginning
of the novel we perceive Updike's need to place his protagonist
against a very specific background, not just any background,
but one which is nationally relevant and realistic. This is clearly
indicative of an ideological preference, for he not merely histo-
ricizes events, piling them up as curiosities worth contemplating
by nostalgic minds, but he, especially, attempts to come to a

synthesis of the different social, scientific, economic, cultural, and political phenomena acting upon the minds, influencing and determining the actions, attitudes, views, and ways of the average American during a specific time in history.

The search for this average American is certainly no easy task, for it implies a search for the typical in a world of great diversity. Nevertheless, Harry (Rabbit) Angstrom is a creation of this attempt to define the forces which bind and boggle the minds of average American citizens and, in the process, reveal history in the making. And the preference of some historical events and aspects over others is obviously not arbitrary; they have been carefully selected, contextualized, and reconstructed so as to serve the purpose of ideological consistency and artistic tension. Static as Rabbit is, in his function as a social common denominator, embodying the fundamental ideological postulates of his country, precise time and space specifications are absolutely essential.

How do we know that *Rabbit, Run* starts on March 20, 1959? We are never told so, directly at least, by the narrator. What we are told through the radio news broadcast is that "Spring [is] scheduled to arrive tomorrow."[1] The next morning, when Rabbit meets Tothero, so we are told, is a Saturday. This would force us to conclude that the novel begins on March 20, a Friday. We are also told that Rabbit, during his flight south, turns on the radio and hears the news that "President Eisenhower and Prime Minister Macmillan [will] begin a series of talks in Gettysburg" (34) and that "Tibetans battle Chinese Communists in Lhasa, the whereabouts of the Dalai Lama, spiritual ruler of this remote and backward land, [being] unknown" (34). Based on this information, we discover that the year is 1959. The records show that, indeed, in 1959 Spring's official arrival was on March 21, Saturday, at 3:55 a.m. The records also show that Prime Minister Macmillan and President Eisenhower met from March 21 to 24 and that the young Dalai Lama was being forced out of Tibet by the invading communist Chinese forces during those very same days. Since March 13, the forces loyal to the Dalai Lama had been fighting the Chinese and on March 23, Indian Prime Minister Jawaharlal Nehru appeals to the Chinese authorities to protect the life and sanctity of the spiritual leader. After various days of uncertainty about Dalai Lama's whereabouts, on March 31, the West is informed by a reluctant Indian Government, apparently trying to do its best to keep out of the conflict, that the Dalai Lama arrived in India. This is all news of the last days of March 1959, so that there is no doubt as to the precise year, month, and day the novel begins.

Updike's choice of actual historic events such as the Dalai Lama's escape, Eisenhower's and Macmillan's meeting should not be taken lightly, unless one naively believes that, indeed, there is such a thing as a neutral or, to use Terry Eagleton's words, a "wholly disinterested [linguistic] statement."[2] Updike's decision to have Rabbit listen to these specific pieces of news on the night of his departure is not a gratuitous act. It serves his purpose of adding representativeness and realism to the hero's mind and actions by making him share the concerns of a rather anonymous voice which speaks not only to him but to a whole community of citizens. And a voice which speaks to a whole community can hardly be said to be purely whimsical. Instead, one would expect it to have a common semantic repertoire and some meaningful message or concern to share with a larger American audience.[3]

That the specific news Updike has his hero listen to is not wholly disinterested can be perceived in that Rabbit's flight and the Dalai Lama's flight are similar in many ways and that political attitudes in America, during this particular time, are in many respects very closely related to the ones Updike chose for Rabbit.

Before reaching his sanctuary in India, the Dalai Lama, like Rabbit, moves south, through mountainous country, nobody knowing of his whereabouts. Also, like Rabbit, he has to avoid "going east, the worst direction, into unhealth, soot, and stink, a smothering hole where you can't move without killing somebody" (29). Had the Dalai Lama moved east he would have landed in the hands of the Chinese; had Rabbit gone east he would have landed in "Baltimore-Washington, which like a two-headed dog guards the coastal route to the south" (34), where

Rabbit believes his freedom is. The east direction is in both cases
an impediment to freedom. For both of them, the south seems
to be a better alternative.

With all these similarities, then, it is not surprising that Rabbit
sees himself as the Dalai Lama. "He is the Dalai Lama" (52), [4] he
tells himself the next day, as he realizes that had "Tothero told
him that they were not going to meet two girls but two goats,
and that they were not going to Brewer but to Tibet [...] not an
atom of his happiness would be altered" (51).

The reader is obviously invited to go on with the analogy, that
is, to somehow equate Brewer with Tibet, that "backward land,"
and Rabbit with the spiritual leader of those backward people.
The ironic undertone of this equation is evident enough, and it
works effectively when one is asked to think of the cross- section
of America as we see it in Mount Judge, Brewer, the conservative
and intolerant Amish community, the economically-guided
Dupont's town and Morgantown, the religious Churchtown, or
the comical Bird in Hand, Paradise, Mt. Airy, Intercourse, and
the like. In an America which in the Fifties sees itself as, and
finds itself at the center of the world,[5] being and perceiving itself
as a power which is being imitated throughout the planet,
Updike's selection of names for his towns, all of them real, works
as ironic, not only because the names are funny in the context
they are presented to us, but also because the names add certain
attributes, a certain schlemielness, to the new nation- hero of
the modern world.

All of these towns are different but in all of them Rabbit sees
some fundamental sameness, and he recalls that "he had
thought, he had read, that from shore to shore all America was
the same. He wonders, is it just these people I'm outside, or is
it all America?" (36). Feeling that even far away from Mount
Judge he cannot feel part of the nation "he climbs into his Ford
distastefully, [and] its stale air is his only haven" (36). Like the
Dalai Lama, Rabbit feels that there is no place for him any longer
in his own country, and, like the Dalai Lama, Rabbit, too, finds
a Sanctuary out of the country, so to speak, since Ruth's style of
life does not conform to the norms which guide the community

of Mount Judge and could very well be taken as "foreign," or at least new, to Brewer.

Other characters have also referred to Harry's sanctity a number of times. Although these references are sometimes clearly jocose and serve more to emphasize Rabbit's schlemielness than a possible sanctity, the fact still remains that these references are numerous and that frequently they are expressed earnestly or at least seem to hide Updike's desire to make us perceive that Rabbit does indeed have saint-like qualities which we should appreciate. As it happens so often with Updike's fiction, its "yes/but quality" is here very evident. Yet, although Rabbit's "sanctity" is doomed to remain controversial, his religiosity — that fundamental characterisitc of Donald Warren's Middle American Radical — is not.

Reverend Eccles's attitude toward Rabbit is perhaps the best example of Updike's attempt to explore Rabbit's religious or "good" side. Although Eccles at first tries to dismiss Rabbit's affirmation that "there is something that wants me to find it" (120) by stating that, "of course, all vagrants think they're on a quest" (120), and that the "little ecstasies" of mystics often "wear a skirt" (121), he soon admits, although still in a somewhat jocose mood, that Rabbit is a better man than he, and that "[Jesus] did say that saints should not marry" (120).

Eccles's seriousness about Rabbit's personal goodness can be seen not only through his dedication but also through his words. With Mrs Springer, Eccles insists that Harry is a "good man" (142), that "by nature [he is] a domestic creature" (146), that "the world he is in now, the world of this girl in Brewer, won't continue to satisfy his fantasies" (146), that "he has to loop the loop" (146) and that he will return.

Because Eccles believes "that Harry Angstrom [is] worth saving and [can] be saved" (156), if only he can take him back to his wife, he decides to appeal to the Lutheran priest, only to discover that, although priests agree that people should be led to salvation, they cannot work together because of their disagreements on the ways of doing so, since Kruppenbach refuses to play the role of the social worker, lawyer, or policeman. On his way to Kruppenbach's home, Eccles reflects that Rabbit has given a special meaning to his golf games; "Harry gives the game a desperate gaiety, as if they are together engaged in an impossible quest set by a benevolent but absurd lord, a quest whose humiliations sting them almost to tears but one that is renewed at each tee, in a fresh flood of green" (157). Much later, in the hospital scene, Eccles seems to understand Rabbit's game-oriented approach to life even better when he states that "as far as [he] can tell the problems of being a baseball player are the same as those of the ministry" (184).

Eccles's increasing respect for Rabbit parallels the reader's, for throughout the book Eccles's observations bring to light the best in Rabbit. This gradual shift from a jocose to a serious mood reaches its highest point when Eccles invites Rabbit to a religious service in his church. The sermon Eccles delivers "concerns the forty days in the Wilderness and Christ's conversation with the Devil" (218). The parallel with Rabbit's flight from Mount Judge and his stay with a prostitute for the last months cannot escape even the most careless of readers.

Rabbit's "sanctity" is also referred to by Mrs Smith and Ruth. Both find, temporarily at least, a new life in him, and both feel abandoned and helpless when he leaves them.

Mrs. Smith, a generally cold, unsentimental, utilitarian, practical old lady, falls deeply in love with Harry as he works in her garden. When Rabbit is reconciled with Janice and has to find a better-paying job, Mrs. Smith confesses: "It's been a religious duty to me to keep Horace's garden up [...] You kept me alive, Harry. It's true, you did" (207). The fact even produces some jealousy on the part of Mrs. Eccles and Ruth.

Ruth pretends to be both surprised and offended by the fact that most people seem to like Rabbit. She claims she cannot understand what he has that makes him so special, although she herself had previously admitted that he was the best lover she had had in a long time, and that his attitude toward the world expresses a fervent desire to live. Her need to discuss the subject seems to stem above all from her fear of losing or having to share her lover with Eccles or Mrs. Smith. Thus, when Rabbit tells her that people like him because he gives them faith (135), Ruth feels compelled to destroy his belief by vulgarizing it and pointing towards his present "incapacity" to support his wife. Her anger at Eccles follows a similar route:

> For the damnest thing about that minister was that, before, Rabbit at least had the idea he was acting wrong but now he's got the idea he's Jesus Christ out to save the world just by doing whatever comes into his head. I'd like to get hold of the bishop or whoever and tell him that minister of his is a menace (139).

Ruth's fear is clearly a fear of the consequences of Rabbit's claim to his own freedom. As she sees it, Rabbit has "it pretty good. [He has] got Eccles to play golf with every week and to keep [his] wife from doing anything to [him]. [He has] got [his] flowers, and [he has] got Mrs. Smith in love with [him]" (134). And he has Ruth, who fears that, should Rabbit's theory about individual freedom be right, she will be the one to pay his price. As Rabbit puts it, "If you have the guts to be yourself, other people will pay your price" (140), a clear indication that he is perfectly aware that his experiment with individual freedom may have consequences which he finds morally unacceptable. Rabbit's flight, although he does not seem to know it, will soon come to an end. He has almost looped the loop, controlled by a social ethic which is no longer willing to grant him his individuality as it is not willing to keep up with what Harry considers acceptable "team" standards.

Rabbit is not recognized as the bearer of a spiritual truth or saint-like traits or behavior by any other of the characters. His orderliness, cleanliness, neatness, sense of justice, courage, wisdom, self- discipline are in fact most of the time ridiculed by the other characters, Tothero being an exception. Even Eccles, as we have seen, in his obsessive attempt to save Rabbit's marriage, cannot fully convince himself that Rabbit's search is genuine rather than a spasmodic and immature gesture of a pretentious vagrant. However, the equation of Rabbit's and the young Dalai Lama's sanctity, although frequently presented to us in a jocose-serious mood is clearly meant as a history-based artistic construct.

Rabbit's triumphal Palm Friday departure and his rediscovery of God on a Sunday morning are so obviously meant to be read as religious symbolism that they have escaped the eyes of few Updike critics. That the news about the Dalai Lama's disappearance should be on the radio broadcasts on a Friday night is also a detail that is both historically accurate[6] (none of the major papers in America published anything about the Dalai Lama on March the 20, but all of them published the news Rabbit refers to, the next day), and a very effective artistic choice made by Updike, forcing, so to speak, a reading of Rabbit as a Dalai Lama — a schlemiel one, it is true, but still one who is likeable, especially for his extreme honesty with himself and others and for his sense of moral responsibility in a world in which the very church which should guide him is faithless and confused about its social role. Rabbit's religiosity, then, expresses one of the most fundamental postulates of the Middle American Radical — a postulate which, despite its different manifestations throughout society, he shares with the rest of America. That despite his confusion Rabbit comes across as quite likeable shows that Updike sees him as possessing qualities (honesty and spontaneity among them) which deserve our appreciation.

Similarly, apolitical as the novel pretends to be, the choice of a piece of news such as the encounter of President Eisenhower and Britain's Conservative Prime Minister Macmillan in Gettysburg is, to say the least, surprising. In fact, the news is perfectly, or almost perfectly, consistent with Updike's representation of Harry's mind as being at one time a participant of and, temporarily, marginal to the nation's political and social atmosphere. The visit of the "vagrant" Prime Minister, described in the papers of the time as "SuperMac" because of his constant travels around the world, had one special meaning — it was meant to solidify the already strong capitalist alliance against Khrushchev's communist Russia. In the agenda was primarily the preparation for a summit of the four world powers (Great Britain, France, the United States, and the Soviet Union) in which the major topic would be the destiny of West Berlin. Lately Khrushchev had unilaterally decided upon a number of measures regarding the access to Berlin — measures which displeased the three powers with control over the city. What Eisenhower and Macmillan had to do was to find a common ground, a common strategy which would allow them to face what throughout the decade had been known as the communist threat. With the Cold War getting hotter every day since 1949, with nationalist movements (consistently perceived as communist-inspired by the Eisenhower administration) spreading all over Eastern Europe, China, Vietnam, Korea, and in many African countries, it would be difficult to understand the total absence of such a concern from the work of a scene- oriented writer like Updike. This piece of news is more, much more, important than one could at first sight imagine. It hides a whole socio-political universe typical of the 1950s, most of which — especially the nuclear threat and the world power conflict — is only present through its conspicuous absence.

Unlike the news on the Dalai Lama, the news on the meeting of these statesmen is slightly and yet meaningfully distorted. The meeting took place in Camp David and not in Gettysburg as Updike's text claims. The question one has to ask is why would an author, so careful about situating his material in space and time, have this discrepancy in the text. Two answers, I believe, are possible. One, is that it is a mistake, a mistake which escaped Updike's revisions, as it actually escaped every single critic; the other that it was a deliberate artistic construct. Updike himself seemed surprised when asked why he had made the two leaders meet in Gettysburg. When informed that they met in Camp David he sounded disappointed and frustrated by what he apparently regarded as a serious flaw. Actually, Eisenhower had indeed been in Gettysburg in those days and news involving the President were generally given as originating in Gettysburg, which I believe explains the mistake. This slip, under the circumstances, however, does little harm to his already consecrated reputation as one of the greatest chroniclers of our time. Judging by the *Los Angeles Times* and *New York Times* of the day, Camp David was quite unknown to most Americans. Both newspapers carry a long, detailed report describing and showing through maps and pictures where Camp David is located and what it looks like. That with all this advertising Updike should have been unaware of the specific location of this conference is surprising but apparently true. This distortion of the geography, done without any deliberate artistic purpose in mind does, however, endow the encounter of the two leaders with a greater national relevance, by creating a symbology reminiscent of Abraham Lincoln's famous "Gettysburg Address," which, I believe, shows that sometimes the wrong way is the better way.

As the text stands, deliberately or not, the Cold War, which the Macmillan-Eisenhower meeting forces us to think about, and Lincoln's Civil War are made to mingle in a pervading imagery of war. These images certainly do not stem only from the mere accidental reference to Gettysburg and the implied private secession from the sacred union of the family and Rabbit's attempt to move south, but especially from the need to select what was selected as news and from the incapacity to avoid the war undertones of the characters' casual daily conversations. So many are the allusions and so many are the direct references to war that it may be but very little exaggeration to call the apparently peaceful *Rabbit,Run* a "war" novel.

Eisenhower and Macmillan are, then, continuing to fight a war which the American public has accepted as its own since the World War II triumph. Updike's selection of such a piece of news is based on the same phenomenon which made a remote, inexpressive and unknown nation like Tibet become relevant to the average American, namely, the fear of communist expansionism. Eisenhower's reliance on the "domino theory" and the accompanying anti-communist propaganda offensive—which, among other things, would lead America into Korea, the disastrous Vietnam adventure, the disastrous invasion of the Bay of Pigs, the invasion of the Dominican Republic and "U.S.-inspired state terrorism in Latin America"[7] and worldwide, had, along with McCarthy's paranoia at the beginning of the decade, been successfully inculcated in the minds of Americans from all segments of society. Although by 1954 McCarthyism would prove to be if not an outright paranoiac creation then the grossest falsification and exaggeration, and was officially pronounced dead, the national fear of the Soviet and Communist threats never seemed to have subsided — an indication that the false accusations had a base of support beyond the individual Joseph McCarthy. McCarthyism was a social phenomenon in America, not an individual caprice. Anti-communism was so deeply associated with American nationalistic feelings that McCarthyism and Joseph McCarthy himself became essential to virtually all political campaigns throughout the country.

It seems that the Eisenhower administration, whose last days serve as the background for Rabbit's story, with a business-oriented Defense Secretary like Charles Wilson, former President of General Motors, had a vested interest in the perpetuation of anti-communist attitudes among the people. Secretary Wilson's blatant statement that he could not conceive of a conflict between his connections with General Motors and his present governmental duties "because for years [he had] thought that what was good for our country was good for General Motors and vice-versa" is indication enough of the close association between big business and the Eisenhower administration. William Whyte, Jr., in his *The Organization Man* (1956), had already called our attention to this attempt to equate the terms America, individual, and corporation. In his view, this was an attempt to do away with a conflict inherent to a healthy social organization, forcing the individual and the country to submit to the ethic of corporations or to what he called simply the "Social Ethic" as opposed to the traditional "Protestant Ethic," whose emphasis was on the individual. The understanding of Updike's selection of news and, for that matter, of Rabbit's story in *Rabbit, Run* largely depends on the understanding of the corporate-oriented anti-communist national mood during the time in which his story takes place.

Similarly, the belligerent Secretary of State, John Foster Dulles, brought over from the Truman Administration, with his foreign policy strategy of "brinksmanship," a policy which "was tested in a number of countries in the fifties"[8] and which, as he put it, consisted of "the capacity to retaliate, instantly by means and places of our own choosing [or of] the ability to get to the verge without getting into the war,"[9] is also a symbol of the anti-communist posture which makes Tibet and MacMillan relevant news to an average American like Harry Angstrom.

This combination of big business and anti-communist national propaganda offensive is even more clearly present in the Taft-Hartley act of 1947. This act, which required anti-communist oaths of all union leaders in the country and which significantly curbed the growing power of the unions, is a vociferous pro-business prelude to McCarthyism.[10]

That the Taft-Hartley act was extended in its application also to employers on the very day, month, and year Rabbit's story begins may be taken as a mere coincidence, but it helps us to do what the novel invites us to do, i.e., to utilize the time referents it offers in order to clearly establish the political climate of those very same days. The new version of the act also confirms that indeed by the late fifties McCarthyism is still more alive than ever and that Senator John Kennedy's and Senator Sam Ervin's proposal to extend the application of the law to the employers asks from big business nothing but a more explicit consistency with the anti-communist posture of the country rather than a change of that posture.

Thus, the selection of news made by Updike, even if attributed to the work of chance, could not have been more fortunate. It not only expresses with remarkable realism the national political worries — it also exposes Rabbit to the concerns that for over a decade have been shared by Democrats, Republicans, workers and employers alike. Although those interests are certainly conflicting in other areas, on this particular issue most of the nation seems to be united, and Rabbit, with his identification with the religious anti-communist Tibetan leader becomes a perfect representative of a typical American attitude of the Fifties. In this respect, one cannot help agreeing with Clinton Burhans's observation that Harry is a victim of a "society from which all escape attempts are frustrated."[11] The conformity on this issue is such that one cannot conceive of Rabbit, through his spasmodic and uncalculated actions, as capable of even considering the possi-

bility of escaping or questioning the social and political struc-
tures of his own society — an attitude which will seriously affect
him, as it will affect America, ten years later in his encounters
with Skeeter. And even twenty years later, when haunted by the
city-wide graffiti claiming that Skeeter lives, Rabbit will experience fear and uneasiness.

Because Rabbit is more a symbol of an average American attitude rather than a genuine expression of the working class, his
is a teleguided mind whose concerns and beliefs have fundamentally been dictated by the dominant ideology of big business. In international terms this can be perceived in his
identification with the concerns of the big-business leaders who
govern the country, especially in his identification with an anti-
communist guru and in his incapacity to question the alleged
(and frequently false) communist threat throughout the globe,
as advertised by his country's leadership, and of which the
Eisenhower-MacMillan encounter is a good example. Nationally
this expresses itself in a basic acceptance of the competitive
world of capitalism in which the agency-centered Rabbit tries,
at all costs, to find a way of employing the advertising techniques he sees on TV and listens to on the radio for improving
his personal performance in his job. His is a struggle more to
recuperate and be accepted by the system rather than a struggle
to change it.

Needless to say that Rabbit in his naivete, as Rachael C. Burchard points out, believes quite blindly in the honesty and integrity of the institutions, at least those of the church, the state, and
the family. He may at times disagree with or be unhappy with
some of their manifestations, but he will never question their
fundamental truths; this is the reason why he feels guilty and
returns, after his spasmodic adventures, not only to his family
but also to his church, to the professional world, and to his life
as a perfect establishment citizen. Rabbit's conservative alliances
resist being undone by three months of absence from the usual
family duties.

With this attitude towards the country's institutions, Rabbit
should feel part of the country and its people; he should feel

that he shares the nation's basic assumptions, and yet, lately, he has felt left out of her, a stranger to her. He senses that he is no longer what he was, the winner, a part of a team of victors, but something else which does not seem to belong to him. But, along with his realization comes our different perception that he shares the concerns, sings the songs, cracks the jokes of his generation, and all its cultural memorabilia, which makes him paradoxical, i.e., both a reflection and a refraction, a mirror-image and a distortion of his decade—a characterization which has nothing to do with the hero- villain controversy in which so many critics have fruitlessly engaged. What one cannot fail to perceive is that the ideological spectrum of *Rabbit, Run* is extremely narrow, and Rabbit's temporary dissension and criticism, like his ill-fated flights, which invariably end only a few blocks away from the starting point, only serve to stress the tacit assumptions which guide the life of his country and which he shares. But his "social ethic" is the ethic of the post-war period, when individual effort and group effort had to coincide, when individual and team victory were one and the same thing. This ethic seems to be falling apart in 1959 when individual pursuits become detrimental to other individuals, for the common goals, the common sense of direction of the earlier years of the decade is gradually dissipating. Like Secretary Charles Wilson, Rabbit, too, thinks, that what is good for him should be good for America. Reality proves to be different.

But, "the class of 51," so we are told, has "learned the same things and gained the same view of life, even in highschools on opposite sides of the city" (56), or on opposite sides of the country. Naturally, this class is familiar with the Cold War, with the great American military success in World War II, with the Korean War, with the nuclear threat, with the need to be prepared for an even greater threat now that the Soviets and communists, so Americans were told, seem to be jeopardizing American hegemony in every corner of the world. World War II, then, marks not only the beginning of a Post-war era, it also marks the beginning of post- war localized, and yet global, wars, with American involvement in virtually every corner of the earth, from Iran to

Guatemala, from Berlin to Greece to Indochina. The world, divided in two, became a stage on which the superpowers started belligerently reenacting the Tordesillas Treaty between Portugal and Spain, four centuries later. Rabbit and the class of 51 grew up in this atmosphere.

Thus, the class of 51, to which Ruth also belongs, is a war-minded generation. It was educated by a generation which fought a war which, because of its awful power of destruction, many feared would be man's last. Ruth expresses this war-mindedness through an almost childish need to win and recognize winners and through the almost absolute meaninglessness she attributes to Rabbit's war preparation experience in the Army. When Rabbit, in the Chinese-Restaurant scene, states that "Chinese food in Texas is the best Chinese food in the United States, except Boston" (60), the following dialogue ensues:

> "You were never in Texas," she says.
> [...]
> "Absolutely I was."
> "Doing what?"
> "Serving Uncle."
> "Oh, in the Army; well that doesn't count. Everybody's been to Texas with the Army" (61).

Ruth's attempt to commonize Rabbit's experience also commonizes the experience of most Americans of his age and older. Indeed, so many of them had been called to serve Uncle Sam during World War II and then "more than a million Americans served in Korea,"[12] and many more served in Indochina and other hot spots throughout the world. The Army experience, Ruth tells us, because it has become so common, has lost its status, so that it "doesn't count" as a man's valuable or distinguished experience, even though it may take you to Texas and to Chinese restaurants. Rabbit's jealousy of Ruth in this same scene confirms the ordinariness of Army life for American men, as "he is irritated by all these Army veterans Ruth seems to know" (61). It is remarkable that they have just met and that Ruth has made no reference to her affairs with Army veterans, to Russian chess- players, or to New York ballet dancers, for that matter. Harry, like Ruth, assumes that Army veterans are everywhere, and he takes it to mean that they must as well have been to bed with the woman sitting next to him.

Ruth, however, seems to be in love with the uncommon thing she sees in Harry's common experience, namely the fact that he still retains the Army spirit, that he has not become "veteranized," that in his "stupid way [he is] still fighting" (89). Ruth is suggesting or saying that most people have stopped fighting and that Rabbit in a way is special, different from most Americans, because the virtue of the fighter is still with him. The extent to which Ruth's sentence expresses the text's ideology — the Hamiltons would obviously disagree — can be seen in our appreciation of Rabbit's refusal in *Rabbit, Run* to accept the kind of life reserved for him in Mount Judge. His flights become a special form of resistance against the surrounding social environment, which, because of its deadness has only room for veterans who stopped fighting. It is this deadness of Mount Judge which makes his flights seem somewhat legitimate to Ruth and to the reader, although they are more a result of post-war nostalgia, an existing spasmodic, glandular energy which has to be expressed, rather than of a clear sense of direction or purpose. It also places Harry's behavior inexorably at the beginning rather than at the end of the decade.

Not without significance are Mr. Angstrom's allusions that the Army is responsible for Rabbit's incapacity to adjust to a "normal" Mount-Judge family life. Mr. Angstrom's associations are that the Army was a negative experience, because it stimulated adventurism, created lack of discipline, destroyed the sense of responsibility for the family and the home. According to him, the fact that Harry "came home and didn't want to get dirty" (152), or that he came "back from the Army and all he care[d] about [was] chasing ass" (152) is the Army's fault. Thus, the hen-pecked husband's and the prostitute's view of the Army do in fact complement each other. Both take the Army spirit, as it should be, seriously, but whereas Mr. Angstrom takes it that the Army has destroyed and failed to give the young people what it should — discipline, desire to fight, respect for the institutions, Ruth still sees the dedicated, disciplined fighter in Rabbit, something which she cannot see in the other veterans the Army has created. And that is what she thinks makes him special, his having retained a quality of the post-war days which is slowly disappearing.

Ruth's assessment, then, is that Rabbit quite accurately represents the ideal, not the actual, fighting spirit of the Army, although her proximity to Rabbit does not allow her to perceive that his present "adventures" do not express a well-grounded refusal of regimentation and the individual's submission to group behavior and group determinations. Because Ruth is incapable of this discernment, she cannot understand Harry's individualism and her feelings toward him become ambiguous. Not surprisingly, therefore, we find her in agreement with Mr. Angstrom. She, too, believes that Rabbit is an irresponsible husband and father, while, simultaneously, admiring him for his uniqueness and his reproduction of an idealized Army spirit she admires. That this spirit can still be found in the 1959 rhetoric of top American officials, who continue to promote Truman's Cold War, makes Rabbit's posture, who "in his stupid way is still fighting," at one time nostalgic and extremely contemporary, while simultaneously pointing towards Rabbit's unbreakable attachment to the sacredness of established powers.

Rabbit's temporary "anti-regimentation" attitude expresses itself, however, less in the Army — in fact, we learn next to nothing about it, and what we learn in *Rabbit Redux* is that he wished he had been sent to Korea — than in his refusal to reenact Mr. Angstrom's attitude of male resignation. Rabbit's refusal to succumb to Janice's way of life, which denies the development of his individuality, seems to confirm Harrison's and Tothero's observation that "Harry is not a team player," as a number of critics have pointed out. Unless the whole team plays so as to adapt to his personal qualities, Harry seems to find no place in it. Harry's outstanding dedication found in Tothero a sensitive coach willing to apparently adapt the tactics and structure of the team to Harry's ability, suggesting that a winning team cannot be victorious without meeting the needs of the individual. We are again invited to see the nostalgic post-war all-embracing

unanimity—a mood so powerful that, although social, structural, collective America had become central, individuality could
still be absorbed. It is the "individualism within organization
life" which William Whyte, Jr. believed ideal. Tothero, the dead
hero, seems to stand for the last efforts and hope to keep individual excellence available to the collective interest. Rabbit's
return to Tothero is not only a search for individuality, however.
Along with it, is the attempt to recover the team, the winning
team, victory, something that for him as for America belongs to
the recent past, and which probably was reawakened by his
experience in the army, an experience which is definitely placed
as the turning point of his life by both his father and his mother.

Rabbit's decision to leave his wife and her way of life is by
comparison a much braver act than Mr. Angstrom's and Mr.
Springer's decision to annihilate themselves under their domineering wives. By contrast, Rabbit's flight is a form of fight. But,
it is only superficially so. Mrs. Angstrom's insight that "[Rabbit]
is just like his father underneath" (150), i.e., not a fighter, pre-
pares us for Rabbit's return to Janice. It not only denies Ruth's
assessment of Rabbit's virtues, it also stresses that his fight,
superficial though it be, is against the world, almost impossible
to win. Janice, the abandoned wife, despite her sloppiness, "has
everybody on her side from Eisenhower down." And, as Mrs.
Angstrom puts it to Eccles, "they'll talk him around. You'll talk
him around" (151). William Whyte, Jr. seemed to be talking
about Harry Angstrom when three years before *Rabbit, Run* was
published he wrote that current organizational trends left little
hope for the individual. His chances of escape, as he saw it,
existed but were minimal. "He may tell the boss to go to hell,"
he wrote, "but he is going to have another boss, and unlike
heroes of popular fiction, he cannot find surcease by leaving the
arena to be a husbandman ....Either he must succumb, resist
them, try to change them, or move to yet another organization."[13] Harry, with his mind placed in the past, resists but eventually succumbs to the impositions of the present.

Eisenhower's name in the sentence above may sound totally
capricious at a first reading. The fact is that Updike's Mrs. Angs-

trom reveals a remarkable understanding—almost too much for a housewife—of the conformity forced upon the country by the America led by Eisenhower. The essentially domestic and conservative Rabbit, however, is not complaining about conformity or team spirit; his anger is against mediocrity, deadness, sloppiness, poor performance—those things which impede team victory. The demand for conformity at home, one should remember, was such that words like non-conformist and un-American became virtually synonymous. And the machinations and fabrications of the Cold War threats did in fact generate a national conformity which, starting with Eisenhower and his General Motors Secretary of Defense, went all the way down to the church, to small business America, to the working class, so that Mrs. Angstrom's sentence reveals with remarkably clarity the spirit of the decade, showing that even if Rabbit did hide a real fighter underneath his gripes, even if he were questioning what Whyte Jr. sees as a threatening social ethic, the fight would have to end in defeat, in surrender to conformity.

The war motif is also present in Mrs. Smith's conversations with Rabbit. The old lady, while explaining to Rabbit what America looked like before the war, suddenly realizes that, with the commonplaceness of war these last decades, Rabbit might not share with her the same frame of reference:

> "I don't suppose when I say 'the war' you know
> which one I mean. You probably think of that
> Korean thing as the war" (131).

Rabbit's answer that he does know which war she is referring to probably has more significance than one is at first sight willing to give it. For one thing it forces us to think of Harry's age. He was a young man of sixteen at the end of the war, and at eighteen, that is, in 1951, in the team of the "class of 51," he was a celebrity, having like his countrymen, who had just came out of a war, experienced the flavor of victory and glory. Thus, Rabbit's answer to Mrs. Smith helps us place his glorious past in a very specific historical time, revealing to us, in the process, that his glorious days coincide with those of immediate post-war America. One glory is brought through victory in war, the other one through victory in basketball. That both coincide so well and that Rabbit seems to understand very clearly what Mrs. Smith is talking about, suggests that Rabbit's past victories are not only hitoricized in the reader's mind but also in his own. The war motif and the basketball motif are so intimately connected through this historicizing that one cannot help seeing here a deliberate artistic purpose in action.

Mrs. Smith's revelation that her son was killed in World War II and her unusual lack of sorrow about her son's death will profoundly influence Rabbit, although only in *Rabbit Redux* this will be perceived. By then Rabbit, an ardent supporter of the Vietnam War, has become as unsentimental about the deaths of American soldiers as Mrs. Smith is now about her son or about her garden in general. Paradoxically, however, now that Mrs. Smith has a substitute son with her — Rabbit would be about the age of her dead son — she feels great affection for him, the same way Rabbit, when faced with the prospect of having his son Nelson sent to Vietnam in a few years, is distressed at the possibility. For both of them war, despite the pain it causes to real people, is necessary and has to be fought by real people, for war is not only a national issue, soldiers doing their duty, fighting for their country, it also has the personal, familial dimension, for the soldier is always a son exposed to danger, a nationalized interest which never quite ceases to be personal.

But, Mrs. Smith also tells Rabbit that "[World War II] was a good war. [...] It was ours to win, and we won it. All wars are hateful things, but that one was satisfying to win" (131). Later, in *Rabbit Redux*, Rabbit will have a similar stance in relation to the Vietnam war, although Mrs Smith herself, judging from her ridicule of the Korean War, would probably have regarded it as a "bad" war, since both were wars fought with the same official justification, namely, that it was being fought against communist expansionism.

The implication of Mrs. Smith's statement is that all wars should be won, although some are "satisfying to win" whereas others may, one imagines, cause certain national discomfort. Whatever the specific references Mrs. Smith had in mind, (is she parroting the official version that World War II was a People's War?) it is remarkable to perceive how the need to win is central to her thought as it is to Rabbit's, Tothero's, and Ruth's. This acquires greater meaning when we remember that it was in the early sixties that Vince Lombardi's famous maxim — "winning isn't everything, it's the only thing" — became so widely accepted in American life. It is also not surprising to see a theologian like Michael Novak, even as late as the seventies, exploring the metaphysics of winning and basing his argument on, precisely, Vince Lombardi's maxim. [14]

The extent to which war and the need to win are associated in Tothero's mind, for example, is not difficult to determine. Rabbit's coach sounds like a general, a commander-in-chief, to whom winning and being successful in life or in a sport are one and the same thing, for "a boy who has had his heart enlarged by an inspiring coach [...] can never become, in the deepest sense, a failure in the greater game of life" (62) Although Tothero tries to convince his small audience that "achievement" can also exist "even in defeat" (62), his attempt to establish this distinction in fact only establishes the norm that winning is achieving, "the only thing," and that if defeat means achievement it is so only in the sense that one achieves the realization that "one's competitors are superior." Thus, Tothero's preference for the word "achievement" is nothing but a euphemism used for self-aggrandizement. Even Tothero himself, while talking to his "friends," perceives that he is being pompous and exaggeratedly rhetorical, so much so that he has to end his little speech with the jocose-religious "and now may the peace of God, et cetera..." (62). Thus, winning, for a coach and for a player, is presented to us in a way not different from Skeeter's view of the American role in Vietnam ten years later, i.e., as a structural determination, a natural thing to do, regardless of one's merits or deserts. Asking them not to win a game is like asking a general and his soldiers not to win a battle. The very consideration in a serious game or a serious war is insane. Either one tries to win it, or the game's very nature is distorted. Although Mrs. Smith would probably recommend that certain wars should be avoided because of their moral justifications, or their lack of popular support, she cannot conceive of suggesting that a war should not be won. Some may be more "satisfying to win" but all should be won once one engages in them. Since wars are started by heads of states rather than by the Rabbits of this world, middle Americans are only left with the pragmatics, the purpose having been set for them. Tothero's view and Rabbit's view are exactly the same on this issue. And, because Tothero and the Army represent crucial moments in Rabbit's life, they have to be seen as directly related to each other.

Thus, Rabbit is immersed in the belligerent and game-oriented mentality of his surrounding environment. His need to return to his former coach, after his flight from Mount Judge, can and must be read as a need to recapture those values which have guided his life until very recently. Tothero's speech reminds us of an Army general. He talks about intellect, body, and heart, of strategy, strength, and determination to win—all attributes of a great basketball player but also attributes essential to a good soldier and to a successful citizen. Under erasure, in manuscript # 169 of *Rabbit, Run*, for instance, Tothero uses words like "ballistics" and "shooting," indicating that in Updike's mind the army general and the basketball coach play very similar roles. What has happened to Rabbit is that he has taken Tothero's idealizations and tried to keep them alive in a society which on the one hand stresses distinction and awards him medals for his outstanding feats as a basketball player and, on the other hand, demands team conformity, ideological regimentation, and tolerance of mediocrity. Thus, while trying to develop those "three tools we are given in life: the head, the body, and the heart" (61), Rabbit is cherishing the rewards which his society in its own idealization of itself also cherishes, as can be seen by its need to keep records and advertise Rabbit's stardom.

In this embodiment of society's underlying idealization of itself, Rabbit resembles Joseph Conrad's Jim who, though common, cannot conceive of himself as ordinary or common. Like Jim, Rabbit cannot accept a life in which the tools of life are not developed to their full potential. Thus, Rabbit trains himself to perfection, painstakingly compensating for his limitations by nourishing his special skills. After breaking the highschool record, he manages to break his own record and keeps it for four years. A truly heroic deed, but one which highlights less his individuality than the pragmatism and the need to win of his milieu.

But one should also remember that this way to achievement is rooted in the tradition of paragons of individuality such as Thomas Jefferson and Benjamin Franklin. Rabbit's practice time-table and Franklin's and Jefferson's daily agendas are directly comparable in the amount of individual energy and dedication they require. Rabbit's mother, therefore, only confirms that Rabbit is moved by this greater idealization when she says that, although "people now say how lazy Hassy is, [...] he is not. He never was. They don't know how hard he [has] worked. Out back every evening banging the ball way past dark [...] when he set his mind to something, there was no way of stopping him. He wanted to be the best at that and I honestly believe he was" (152). Thus, it is Rabbit's personal determination—a determination stemming from a Protestant ethic rooted in the American dream—which makes him extraordinary. In his way, through sports, he makes come true those idealizations cherished by his fellowmen. One thinks of the self-made man, Emerson's self-reliance, Thoreau's civil disobedience, and similar individual gestures which in the corporate world of the fifties had become little more than a romantic ideal, worthy to be celebrated when transformed into achievement but something to be controlled, feared perhaps, at a time when corporate conformity, although dominant, is beginning to show signs of weakness, paving the way to the trouble land of the sixties. For Rabbit, however, the temporary independence is always overshadowed by his sense of commitment to a first-rate life within the structure of team and marriage.

Janice's unwillingness to join him in this venture and her lack of sympathy for his plight stimulate his need to find "that thing that wasn't there." The real around him has to be changed to become bearable; the way it is, it is a losing game. When playing basketball or golf, Rabbit cannot remove his eyes from where the ball should go, the ideal. Only if the ball reaches the intended goal can he be a winner, happy. Similarly, one may infer, only when Janice stops drinking, smoking, stops being sloppy, only when she can communicate with him, when she takes care of her body, when she becomes a good cook, a good lover, when television becomes less important, only when she can empathize with the plight of his professional life, only then can he be a winner and live a happy life.

Not surprisingly, even his old coach, Tothero, at a time of required conformity, can no longer allow Rabbit to play his individual game. Tothero, who had at first taken Rabbit for a spree, who told him to "do what the heart commands" (53), who had called Janice a "little mutt" (55), still regards Rabbit's return to Janice a necessity, the adult thing to do. His, too, is a message of conformity. As with Eccles, for Tothero, unity at home, even when the marriage is bad, is a sacrament and has to be preserved at all costs. The fact that Tothero's name reminds one of a dead hero and the fact that by the end of the novel he is half-paralyzed are possible indications of Updike's concern with the all-embracing organizational ethic of the fifties, which on the one hand stresses conformity, re-union, and, on the other hand, rewards individual achievement. The paralyzed half, with which Rabbit seems to identify more strongly during his two-month adventure, however, stands for the individual manifestations, the negative text of America in the fifties.

Rabbit, Run does not introduce topical events beyond those to which I referred, but the socio-economic life and the religious trends, with which Rabbit has to cope, show that Rabbit is indeed a creature of the fifties. Rabbit reacts to these forces but fails to define his goals or to achieve a clarity of purpose, the reason why Charles Child Walcutt calls Rabbit's movement "centripetal." This kind of trajectory is very similar to Rabbit's jogging in the seventies, as Thomas Mallon pointed out in an article in the *National Review* (1981) called "Rabbit, Jog." The implication of this movement is that Rabbit is not really running away from but rather running to and fro like a jogger who knows that the end of his journey is at the point of departure. This is more clearly perceived with the knowledge of what happens to Rabbit in *Rabbit Redux,* and *Rabbit is Rich,* an aspect which significantly affects the reading of the novel, for it confirms our conclusion that Rabbit's is an essentially conservative mind.

Rabbit's domesticity, however, is evident not only in his incapacity to move away from the Mount Judge area, his going back to Tothero, his sacralization of marriage, his return to Janice once he knows she is having his baby, his great attachment to his father, mother, and sister, but also by the other values of the nation which he embodies in their ideal form— pragmatism, religiosity, the sacralization of authority, anti-communism, and the need to win, —as I have already pointed out. Similarly, his domesticity can be seen in his attitude toward his job and television, not so much because he identifies with the collective posture of the country, but because his posture, in its ambiguity, reveals the dominant trends of the decade.

It has been pointed out by Kathleen Lathrop that a significant part of Rabbit's discontent has to do with the triviality of his job, first as a kitchen-gadget demonstrator and, later, as a used-car salesman. This is true to a large extent, since Rabbit indeed does not find his job appealing or fulfilling. It is more duty than pleasure. Rabbit's job is in his mind at all moments and, like someone who has developed good personal discipline, he automatically connects everything he sees, hears or feels—advertisements, sentences, observations, jokes, etc. —to the work he has to do. His anger at Janice in the first pages of the book, when they are watching a television program for kids, has to do with "her missing the point of why he wanted to watch Jimmy, for professional reasons, to earn a living to buy sugar for her to put into her rotten old Old-fashioned" (17). A little earlier, "it gripes him that [Janice] didn't see his crack about being a housewife, based on the image the Magi-Peel people tried to have their salesmen sell to, as ironical and at bottom pitying and fond" (17).

Later, in the Chinese restaurant scene, Rabbit tries a similar job-related crack with Ruth:

> "You don't want to talk about your weight, either.
> Huh." [...] "Let's try this. What you need, Mrs.
> America, is the Magi-Peel Kitchen Peeler. Preserve
> those vitamins. Shave off fatty excess. A simple
> adjustment of the plastic turn screw, and you can
> grate carrots and sharpen your husband's pencils.
> A host of uses."
> "Don't. Don't be so funny" (69).

This time it works, forcing us to think that perhaps Ruth has something to offer that Janice no longer has or wants to offer, namely the possibility of communicating. Ruth can at least understand his irony, whereas Janice seems flatly uninterested in empathizing with Rabbit's job-related mind.

As these examples suggest, Rabbit is perfectly willing to get involved with his job. He actually does his best to be the best at it, as if it were a game which, since you are playing it, should be won. When he tells Ruth, in the restaurant scene, that he demonstrates "something called the Magi-Peel kitchen peeler" (62), Tothero, sure that he knows his former athlete better than anybody else, is quick to add:

> "and I'm sure he does it well. [...] I'm sure that
> when the Magi-Peel Corporation Board sits down
> at their annual meeting and ask themselves 'now
> who has done the most to further our cause with
> the American Public?' the name of Harry Angstrom
> leads the list" (62).

This observation of his former coach may be somewhat exaggerated, but the fact that Rabbit can hardly think of anything except in relation to his job, and his need to sell his gadget does seem to indicate that Rabbit, the worker, and Rabbit, the player, are very similar. Both are in constant search for improvement and, to achieve that, hard work, constant attention and training are necessary.

Thus, to say that the major source of Harry's discontent is his trivial job is to attribute to him questioning powers which he does not have and that Updike certainly did not mean for him to have. Rabbit is not unhappy because America has shifted "from a production economy to a service economy"—he is unhappy because he wants to be successful in this service economy and finds nobody who can understand his need to be outstanding, or, put differently, he finds no team which appreciates his effort. Rabbit's tragedy, I repeat, keeping the proper distinctions in mind, is not very different from Willy Loman's in that, although they are average men and have limited equipment to outdo the others in the game of life, both refuse mediocrity. The only life they consider worth living is the life of winners. That both are salesmen and go around doing their best trying to sell their products and themselves is more an indication of their absorption of the values and ways of the system at work rather than an expression of their unhappiness with it. The unhappiness, one infers, is more Updike's and Miller's rather than Rabbit's or Willy Loman's.

Rabbit's job is indeed emblematic of the fifties. For the first time in history, the tertiary sector of the economy became dominant. And as John Kenneth Galbraith noted in his *The Affluent Society*, "in the years following World War II, the American economy, [...] became for the first time an economy of abundance, producing more goods and services than those with money were able to consume."[15] Updike, again, knew what job he was selecting for Rabbit in order to make it historically representative. The gadget is undoubtedly the best representative of a society of abundance, since it stands for the unessential and truly unnecessary. Rabbit himself has insights into this triviality during his aborted trip south, when he sees the weathered billboards along the road, advertising all sorts of "products you wondered anybody would ever want to buy" (37).

But recognizing the triviality of his gadget does not lead him to question the system which has made it "necessary." Instead, like Donald Warren's Middle American Radical, he is willing to work hard in order to be able to enjoy what the system has to offer. Rabbit, like the average American of his day, takes the system as a given and believes that he can make it ideal for himself through personal effort. Labor relations, for example, don't ever cross Rabbit's mind, and if they did, in all likelihood, he would have dismissed the topic as too political, for as we learn during his first day with Tothero he gets quite easily

"depressed by the political air of the place" (21). In other words,
Rabbit's discontent in *Rabbit,Run* is not caused by the economic
structure of American society but by his belief that he could excel
within the structure if some basis of support could be found
among those closest to him. Here, Rabbit is definitely not like
the Harvard undergraduates Kenneth Keniston talks about in
his book *The Uncommitted: Alienated Youth in American Society*
(1965), a book which serves as the basis for so many discussions
on *Rabbit, Run*. Updike went to Harvard — Rabbit did not. We
should not confuse the problematizations of an intellectual elite
with the spasmodic doings of a middle American.

This belief in the system is what makes Rabbit domestic, average, ordinary, emblematic, a reflection of the dominant forces of
the decade, and a reformist. What makes him refractive, different but not revolutionary, is his long-lasting and decisive belief
that the individual can succeed, excel, and reach perfection, as
he once did. In Rabbit's mind, as with corporate America, the
system is always determined by the individual and not the other
way around. It worked for him with Tothero's basketball team —
it has not yet worked for him with America. If indeed "the only
thing you've got in this life is what you can sell," as Charley tells
Willy Loman in *Death of a Salesman*, then Rabbit's frustrations
have to do with the gadgets and with his lack of qualifications
for life within the economic system. As a basketball player he
had his valuable skill to sell and he could persuade Tothero to
"buy" it. As a gadget salesman he cannot, as easily, bend the
system to his advantage, for what he sells, even if people buy
it, never ceases to be somewhat superfluous, a superfluousness
which extends itself from producer to consumer, leaving Harry
with the unpleasant feeling that he is operating as a mediating
link between these two poles of waste. That he never manages
to rationalize his feelings and engage them in a calculated social
reaction only demonstrates Updike's intention to preserve his
middleness.

The effects of the economy on Rabbit can also be seen in the
widespread use of the car, in the tremendous expansion of the
freeway system, and in the advertising boom. All of these forces

corroborate my views about Rabbit's favorable attitudes toward the system.

The automobile absolutely dominates the novel. Even "the darkness vibrates with the incessant automobile noises" (42). The last drop in the full cup of Rabbit's and Janice's conflicts is their car. It is when Rabbit goes to pick up the car, which Janice had left at her mother's, that he decides to flee.

He crosses a city dominated by street lights and enters a maze of freeways that so confuse him that even with the help of a map, he loses his way. The freeway system that we have in *Rabbit, Run* works as a web on which Rabbit is forced to "tread" if he wants to flee, and yet this same web is so labyrinth-like that he ends up where he began, caught in it.

The car economy, along with its freeways and its consequent suburbs, shopping centers, drive-ins, parking lots, and gas stations, affects Rabbit directly as it did most Americans of the time,[16] and Rabbit does show some temporary signs of unhappiness. This can be easily perceived in this description of what Rabbit sees of Brewer early in the morning, as he returns by car, after his first aborted attempt to flee. The words are the narrator's, but his closeness to Rabbit is such that we have to make the words of one the other's:

> He comes into Brewer from the south, seeing it in the smoky shadow before dawn as a gradual multiplication of houses among the trees beside the road and then a treeless waste of industry, shoe factories and bottling plants and company parking lots and knitting mills converted to electronics parts and elephantine gas tanks lifting above trash-filled swampland yet lower than the blue edge of the mountain from whose crest Brewer was a warm carpet woven around a shade of brick (41).

It is passages like this which make Larry Taylor's anti-pastoral findings sound extremely reductionistic— not because there is no anti-pastoral satire in *Rabbit, Run*, but because of the tremendous anti-urban force of Updike's text. The cars, the freeways, the parking lots, the industrial world have transformed and destroyed the natural landscape so much that even what remains of Eden, like Mrs. Smith's garden, described as a heaven on earth, is being controlled by cold, pragmatic, and utilitarian minds.

Furthermore, there are strong indications that the quasi-pastoral is preferred by Rabbit over his gadget world. The same way he prefers to remove all that is artificial, all gadgets and cosmetics from Ruth's body before making love, he also feels quite happy with his simple and unskilled job in Mrs. Smith's garden. It is an impossible paradise to live in if one has "promises to keep," a wife and a child to feed, but still Rabbit leaves it not because he dislikes it but because, simply, he needs money to support his family. Unhappily for him, the world of the gadgets, used and new cars, and freeways still pays better, and he is forced to go back.

It should also be noted that Rabbit, despite the negative associations with the car, also recognizes some need for it. His decision to return his car to Janice has nothing to do with his dislike for its omnipresence; he takes his car back to her because, (1) he has to admit that it is half hers anyway, and (2) he decides that she needs it more than he does right now.

The fact that Rabbit uses his car to flee, accepts car lifts without second thoughts, recognizes that a car can be a necessity for others, and finally accepts his father-in-law's offer to work in his lot as a used-car salesman—all this seems to indicate that even if the car's omnipresence irritates Rabbit and contributes to the destruction of the natural landscape, he is incapable of categorically refusing its world. This ambiguity is the ambiguity of the decade as well as of Rabbit's. It reveals the coexistence of two texts in the American society of the period, two texts which had been in conflict with each other at least since the first train, like a Trojan horse with its belly full of greedy merchants, to use Thoreau's imagery, traveled across the American landscape. The urban and industrialized world had become dominant earlier in American society, but the fifties, with its post-war industrial boom, affirmed this dominance more than ever. In this world, Rabbit's dilemma is solved more by necessity than by choice. The irreversibility of the system makes the choice for the indi-

vidual regardless of his desires. Despite his momentary flirtations with the bucolic, and despite his realization that it is sadly
disappearing, his final behavior is that of a man of the establishment, affirming the dominant text and justifying it through the
style of life which he has been told is necessary for the progress
of the modern world.

The impact of television on Rabbit's life in *Rabbit, Run* is also
enormous. There is hardly a page in the novel which does not
contain a direct or indirect reference to it. The medium invades
Rabbit's home and Rabbit's mind, entertaining, preaching, and
selling. Television is an integral part of the novel's intrigue, for
Rabbit's mind, despite his momentary rebellions, finds there its
matrix. He walks around Brewer with distorted television messages in his mind the same way Leopold Bloom walks around
Dublin turning his advertising jingles in his head.

For most part, it seems that Rabbit resents the medium, realizing perhaps that his video-maniac wife finds it more interesting than him. When Rabbit arrives home, he finds his wife Janice
"watching television turned down low" (12) with "vague dark
eyes reddened by the friction of watching" (13). Communication
between them is barely possible, and television, instead of offering a common source for discussion actually generates conflicts.
In fact, television seems to be at the very center of their quarrels.
Later in the book, when Rabbit tells Janice why he left, we discover that television was one of the main reasons. He tells her:

> "Well Jesus Janice. All you did was watch televi-
> sion and drink all the time. I mean I'm not saying I
> wasn't wrong, but it felt like I had to. You get the
> feeling you're in your coffin before they've taken
> your blood out" (199)

The explanation could not be clearer: he was running away
from a second-rate life—something which he finds unbearable
after having been "first-rate at something" (101). And this second-rate life is television-centered. Television not only keeps
closet doors half-closed, but it also forces Rabbit to keep his
mouth half-closed. Even after almost three months away, when
Rabbit visits with Janice in the hospital, Rabbit is asked to turn

on the coin-operated television in her bedroom. Janice's addiction, so it seems, has made her know the daily programs by heart. Needless to say that Rabbit feels, and rightly so, that his visit is less important than the daily program.

It is also necessary in this context to recall that Rabbit's main words of "wisdom" — words which are at the center of his "theological" discussions with Eccles — come from television, actually from a program for children. God, he learns from TV and tells Eccles, does not want "a waterfall to be a tree" (101). Eccles turns this sentence around and gives it back to Rabbit as, "but I think he wants a little tree to become a big tree" (102), suggesting that what Rabbit needs is to grow. Rabbit perceives that he is being seen as immature and, although he is willing to accept the charge, he is unwilling to recognize any validity in what Eccles seems to see as the mature world. His reply is swift and direct:

> "If you're telling me I'm not mature, that's one
> thing I don't cry over since as far as I can make out
> it's the same as being dead" (102).

This controversy can be said to have its roots in the Mouseketeer's synonymization of "know thyself" and "be yourself," as most critics would agree. The synonymization makes Rabbit perceive himself as unique, as an individual, as different from others, and he begins placing greater and greater value on his individuality.

This outburst of individuality triggered by Jimmy, the big Mouseketeer, generates, if not self-knowledge, then at least some self-realization of the quality of his life. Rabbit does realize that the way he lives is "the same as being dead" (101) and that the "stubborn smallness" (55) of Janice is unbearable. Added to his sister Mim's confirmation of this deadness, when she introduces him to her boyfriend — "This is my brother [...] he's back from the dead" (169) — we have, in this temporary refusal to join the masses, a nice piece of social criticism.

Considering that during the fifties children spent an average of five hours a day in front of a television set[17] and considering that Rabbit can hardly stand television's interference in his family life, we could infer that Rabbit is not a reflection of his decade but a freak who swims against the current. This is only partly true.

First, as we have seen, Rabbit is largely exposed to the medium as everybody else is. He watches it for words of wisdom which he believes can help him with his life and his professional career. Thus, it seems that he is more in conflict with the addiction of his wife and its interference in their relationship than with the medium itself. As *Rabbit Redux* and *Rabbit is Rich* confirm, his reaction against TV is again not that of a conscious objector, only another spasm which the system will soon manage to control.

Furthermore, it is remarkable and ironic that Harry's explosion of individuality should be generated by the very medium which by its nature brings sameness to the country. This choice of having a collective medium, the same which the establishment utilizes for commercial advertising and its political propaganda, produce a distorted anti-establishment view stresses perhaps the strength of the system and its capacity to tolerate minor deviations. Meanwhile, the Rabbits of this world are left with false illusions about the tolerance and flexibility of the system. As Noam Chomsky puts it, "the democratic system of thought control is seductive and compelling. The more vigorous the debate, the better the system of propaganda is served, since the tacit, unspoken assumptions are more forcefully implanted."[18] In other words, you can be yourself as long as your goals are the system's. But, because individual and social interests are so frequently at odds with each other, Rabbit's "be yourself" is as much a blunder as Secretary Charles Wilson's "what is good for General Motors is good for America." That Rabbit's contentions with the system are teleguided demonstrates the extent to which his life is not really his. His disagreements with the establishment are cosmetic rather than structural, and it should be no surprise to find Rabbit ten years later with an American flag stuck to his car or twenty years later reading hardly anything except *Consumer Reports*.

Whether through his exposure to topical events or through a description and characterization of the milieu, Rabbit becomes an epitome of his decade, reflecting both the positive and the negative texts of the period. His conflicts, however, whether with family life, his job, television, cars, freeways, industrialization, acquaintances, or with his present self—all are spasmodic, cosmetic, and superficial. The teleguided nature of his life does not allow for conflicts which are more profound. Yet the superficiality of the conflicts does not make them less real or representative. The fifties, which have come to be known in America as the decade of economic abundance and social and political conformity, already contain the spark which in the sixties will set the house of middle Americans on fire. The temporary irritations in Rabbit's body and mind, however, has to be seen as the itching caused by the virus which will inoculate him against the anti-establishment manifestations of the sixties. *Rabbit Redux* is a splendid study of this and other viruses which will affect the health of the nation.

Notes

[1] John Updike, *Rabbit, Run* (New York: Fawcett Crest, 1960) 34. All further references to this novel are cited parenthetically in the text.

[2] Terry Eagleton, *Literary Theory—An Introduction* (Minneapolis: University of Minneapolis Press, 1983) 13.

[3] In an article entitled "The Artist and His Audience," published in *The New York Review* on July 18, 1985, Updike argues that the artist always wants to please his audience: "the creative imagination wants to please its audience, and it does so by sharing what is most precious to it. A small child's first instinct vis-a-vis possessions is to hug what it has tight to itself..." In *Picked-up Pieces* (1966) Updike had already worked on this same idea: "I have described the artistic transaction as being between the awakening ego and the world of matter to which it awakes; but no doubt the wish to please one's parents enters early, and remains with the artist all his life, as a desire to please the world, however displeasing his behavior may seem, and however self-satisfying the work pretends to be (In John Updike, *Picked-up Pieces* (New York: Fawcett Crest, ed. 1975) 50. If the radio broadcaster is, like the writer, "an instrument, a means whereby a time and a place make their mark," then we can say that the relationship between the speaker and listener has more to do with harmony than with tension, more with confirmation than with disruption of an audience's expectations.

[4] Updike's first manuscript of *Rabbit, Run* shows that significant research went into the the the selection of the pieces of news for the radio broadcast Rabbit hears on his way to West Virginia. The manuscript is interrupted, with a little less than half a page of blank space reserved for the news. Only in the second

draft do we have the text of the radio broadcast inserted, indicating that Updike wrote it only after he had made sure its information was accurate, representative, and meaningful.

[5] A ten-page long article published in *U.S. News and World Report*, on March 23, 1959 is a good popular example of this perception. The article is entitled "Is the World going American?" This is the article's lead: "America's biggest export boom is now under way. But you can't put a cash value on it—yet. The exports are intangibles: American ideas, methods and habits. They are being adopted all over the world, changing the lives of people of all ages, in all walks of life. It's a sort of American revolution" sweeping the globe. This acceptance of U.S. ways of doing things—in industry, in business, in homes—comes by free choice at a time when Communists are competing for men's minds. Regional Editors for "U.S. News & World Report," in posts around the world, give you firsthand accounts of U.S. influence at work, showing how people abroad copy American ways and reject Soviet patterns of life" (74). Propaganda or not, the article does show America's presence and influence throughout the globe, along with an American perception of itself as a center of world influence. The anti-communist tone is an essential aspect of this perception.

Updike's own awareness of this American influence in the world is repeatedly expressed. In "The American Man: What of Him?", for example, he writes: "All over the world, coolies and fakirs are picking themselves up out of the age-old mire and asking, "How can we become like Yanqui men?" Our State Department, cleansed of intellectual southpaws, works night and day on the answer" In *Assorted Prose* (New York: Alfred Knopf, 1974) 4.

Kenneth Keniston's study on alienation among Harvard undergraduates in the fifties also indicates that, considering the general affluence of America, it is difficult to understand the widespread rejection of the system, when youngsters throughout the world fight to have the very same benefits and privileges that American youngsters are rejecting. This was one of the reasons which led Keniston to see alienation in America as taking the form of "rebellion without a cause, of rejection without a program, of refusal of what is without a vision of what should be." Kenneth Keniston, *The Uncommitted—Alienated Youth in American Society* (New York: Harcourt, Brace & World, Inc., 1960) 6.

[6] The frontpage headlines of the *New York Times* and *The Los Angeles Times* on March 19 and March 20 refer to atomic experiments and to anti-Soviet military action. These are the major headlines in the *New York Times* on March 19: "U.S. Army orders a missiles group to West Germany;" "U.S. Atom Blasts 300 miles up Mar Radar, Snag Missile Plan; Called 'Greatest Experiment';" "Test created curtain of Radiation around the earth for a short time." The frontpage headlines in *The New York Times* on March 20 were not very different: "Quarles says atom shots aided weapons research in attack and in defense;" "Moscow agrees to parley May 11 but limits topics" (wants talks confined to the Berlin and Germany issue); "Non-communist employer oath favored by senate committee."

[7] Noam Chomsky, *Toward a New Cold War* (New York: Pantheon Books, 1982) 51.

[8] Jeffrey D. Merrit, *Day by Day: the Fifties* (New York: Facts on File, 1979) xi.

[9] Ibid. p. xi.

[10] *Dictionary of American History* (New York: Charles Scribner's Sons, 1976) 456-57.

[11] Clinton Burhans, "Things Falling Apart: Structure and Theme in *Rabbit, Run,*" *Studies in the Novel,* 5 (1973) 336-51.

[12] Frank N. Magill, ed., *Great Events from History* (Englewood Cliffs, New Jersey: Salem Press, Inc, 1975) 1825.

[13] William Whyte, Jr., *The Organization Man* (New York: Simon and Schuster, 1956) 12.

[14] Michael Novak, *The Joy of Sports: End Zones, Bases, Baskets, Balls, and the Consecration of the American Spirit* (New York: Basic Books, Inc., 1976) 230- 31.

[15] John Kenneth Galbraith, *The Affluent Society.* (Boston: Houghton Mifflin Company, 1958) 123.

[16] "In the 1956 Federal-Aid Highway Act, Congress authorized a major highway construction program, with the federal government paying 90 percent of the costs. Over the next two decades thousands of miles of high- speed multilane highways were thrown across the land, affecting, for better or for worse, the areas through which they passed....The expanded use of the private automobile made [the shopping center] distribution system possible, as acres of parking space that were an integral part of every shopping complex emphasized. The continuing love affair with the automobile was documented by the fact that during the 1950's consumers spent about 5 percent of their disposable income on automobiles and automobile-related products" (Jonson, M. Arthur. "Economy Since 1914." Nathan Rosenberg, *Encyclopedia of American Economic History.*(New York: Charles Scribner's Sons, 1980) 110-29.

[17] The impact of television on American life, starting in the fifties is all pervasive. It affected, among other areas, entertainment, education, communications, the advertising and the business industries, religion, politics, and, obviously, family life. Arthur Johnson points out that "Television replaced radio in the 1950's as the primary home entertainment medium. Black-and-white sets were displaced by color sets in less than a decade. Television became the baby-sitter of a new generation of children who spent more time in front of the family set than in the classroom, absorbing a fast-moving set of images that ranged from the superb to the absurd" Arthur Johnson, "Economy since 1914," In Nathan Rosenberg, *Encyclopedia of American Economic History* (New York: Charles Scribner's Sons, 1980.) 122.

[18] Chomsky, Noam. *Toward a New Cold War.* New York: Pantheon Books, 1973, p. 81.

Chapter 3

The Solid Citizen

"Offhand I'd say we're doing a good enough
business in the jails without putting solid citizens
like you in there"

(Rabbit Redux).

Rabbit Redux opens with an epigraph which to some extent explains the title of the novel. "Redux," we are told, means not only a reconsideration of Rabbit's life, it also means "return to health after disease."[1] The epigraph actually explains little more than the existence of a trajectory between two opposite poles, one healthy, the other sick. But the reader may at times find it difficult to identify the starting point and the end of this trajectory. Most of the time, however, one has little or no doubt that sick is the world Harry has been living in these last ten years, and healthy is the experience he and his wife go through while exposed to a number of "reality instructors" — Skeeter, Jill, Mr. Angstrom, Mr. Springer, Mim, and Stavros. These experiences are at times quite conventional but at other times they can be extremely passionate and risky, forcing Rabbit and Janice to start their life anew, if not to begin a new life.

In many ways, Rabbit is not the same anymore. He is fat, has a "thick waist" (14) and is described by his former lover, Ruth, as having "had [his] days in the lettuce patch" (67). In fact, "years have passed since anyone has called him Rabbit" (14). He is now called "Harry" and lives a monotonous life which routinely repeats itself day after day. As he tells Jill, his teenage lover, later in the novel, what he does every day is essentially "set type, watch TV, [and] sit around" (119). His life in "the stagnant city of Brewer" (13) has become so sexless, joyless, that "now there is enough death in him so that in a way he wants to kill" (117).

The last ten years of his life have made him outer-oriented to the extreme, and it takes fights, destruction, and death until he realizes that perhaps indeed his life is not so much his own as

he had imagined. After ten years his numbness has made him
more intensely a faithful and loyal member of the broader
national community to whom television speaks every day and
every night of the year. The Harry who in *Rabbit, Run*, ten years
ago, wondered if he was only a foreigner to Mount Judge or to
the whole country now realizes that, whereas he is marching
according to the drumbeat of the establishment, many others
are out of step, even his wife. Having now lost the disguises of
Rabbit Run, Harry has become an outspoken and perfect expression of society's most conservative values. He openly defends
competitive society, he is a fierce nationalist, he hates communists, blacks, foreigners, and regards women as illogical, inferior, and irresponsible. Although one could say that he has very
little to preserve, he has become a staunch conservative. The
established order is more sacred than ever for him. Like the
"silent majority" with which Janice identifies him, certainly
unaware that Nixon, so Gore Vidal tells us, stole the expression
from Homer, who used it to refer to the dead, he is ready to let
the establishment have its way as long as it tells him that America is great, white, beyond any other power, "a face of God,"
and that "wherever America is not, madness rules with chains,
darkness strangles millions" (49).

And because Harry has become such a loyal nationalist and
such a staunch conservative, he has been quite unhappy with
the present state of affairs in America. Too many Negroes seem
to be "spitting" on him every time he turns on the TV, and,
regarding foreign affairs, he has the feeling that everybody who
opposes the Vietnam War is either a "foreigner" like Stavros, or
a communist. This angers him, and his personal reaction is to
protect the establishment against such destabilizing intruders,
in a way recuperating and rewriting the famous sentence quoted
in "Eisenhower's Eloquence." In that piece, too, Updike
rewrites Eisenhower's "Only Americans can hurt America" as
"Only Americans can understand America. Only Americans
can love America."[2] Similarly, Rabbit perceives criticism of
Administration policies as an unpatriotic act. His Falcon carries
the American flag, a symbol of national unity, no doubt, but for

him, especially, a symbol of identification with the establishment policies. He could not care less if it all means, as his wife's lover puts it, "cops bopping hippies on the head and the Pentagon playing cowboys and indians all over the globe, [screwing] blacks and [sending] the CIA into Greece" (47). Harry's nationalism is largely directed at precisely these three forces of the sixties: hippies, blacks, and foreigners like Stavros, whom he immediately associates with communists or communist sympathizers. Although Janice calls his "flag decal on the back window of the Falcon [...] corny and fascist" (21), Rabbit thinks that this is an effective and necessary way of showing those "draft resisters" who are "taking over the garden" (21) who has the upper hand. America is "his garden" (21) and he wants everybody to know it.

Harry's pro-war stance in the sixties, as we have seen, has its roots in the early fifties. In *Rabbit Redux* we are reminded of his personal frustration for not having been sent to the Korean War (117), so that we can infer that his present behavior is an ideological extension of the earlier decade rather than a rational creation of a new personal set of logical postulates. His conclusions are, as a matter of fact, establishment cliches whose meaning he does not fully control. His anger and evasiveness invariably come to the surface once he runs out of arguments. His justification for the CIA involvement with the Greek dictatorship, for example, is that "the Greeks can't seem to manage the show by themselves" (47)—a version which besides its self-projection (his own home is being invaded by Stavros, and it is worth mentioning that Stavros refers to his affair with Janice as a "rescue mission") can only come from minds which are, deliberately or not, allied to the interests of dominant national groups which support such actions and which, therefore, are able to deny, de facto, other nations and peoples their right to sovereignty.

Harry, as we can see, has not learned to think politics, and he actually boasts that "one of [his] goddamn precious American rights [is] not to think politics" (47), confirming Donald Warren's claim that middle Americans tend to avoid involvement in national politics, preferring to settle for local issues. And, because Harry, like middle America, does not perceive how outer-directed his behavior is, he also does not perceive that his attitude is as political as that of those who oppose the official doctrine. His unconscious support of the dominant national powers not only make him ideologically a member of the status quo but also an accomplice of international and national atrocities. Despite this ideological identification with the dominant powers of the country, the pseudo-rebel of the fifties, because of his labor-class condition, will be a victim of the system which these powers nourish.

Janice's decision to leave Rabbit throws him into situations which will, to a certain extent, change these attitudes of his. After she leaves him, Janice tells Rabbit:

> "It is the year nineteen sixty-nine and there's no reason for two mature people to smother each other to death simply out of inertia. I'm searching for a valid identity and I suggest you do the same" (98).

Rabbit follows her advice. While Janice carries on her affair with Stavros, a son of Greek immigrants and an employee at Springer Motors, Rabbit brings into his home Jill, a "comely lass, raised in the bosom of the middle class" (154), so young that she could be his daughter. Being a representative of the self-marginalized counterculture types of the sixties, Jill openly refuses all the values of the society that brought her up, and which Harry still lives by. She hates its materialism, she hates the capitalist system and its consumerism and oppression, and she even "tends to forget material details like [eating]" (127). Jill finds solace from the society she hates in drugs.

It is largely due to Jill's presence that Harry is, temporarily at least, sexually reborn and learns to be less intolerant of political views, generally less conservative than his own. Jill, too, he discovers, opposes the Vietnam War, besides being a sympathizer of Che Guevara. She passes all these ideas of hers to his thirteen-year-old son Nelson, and Harry with a little uneasiness, but calmly, accepts all this, as if his wife's departure gave him carte blanche to do whatever he pleased, especially the generally forbidden.

When Skeeter, the black Vietnam veteran, is brought into his house, Harry, after a heated altercation, beats him up, and then, surprisingly, allows him to stay. Skeeter passes drugs on to Jill, rapes her in front of Harry, and seems to have him totally under his control. That Harry is able to beat Skeeter up, thus asserting his power over him, and then accept his presence can be read as a demonstration of strength on Harry's part. He seems to be willing to understand Skeeter's rebellion against whites and his views on Vietnam. Skeeter regards the war as absurd and yet as a natural thing for America to do—as natural as a cockroach which "does its cockroach thing" (231). With Skeeter and their group readings on history, culture, and philosophy, Harry realizes for the first time that his ideas are old-fashioned, that certain words and certain ideas were even being used by their old friend Peggy Fosnacht, whom he never regarded as bright. And yet, even she is using expressions that until very recently were forbidden to ordinary people. When Peggy refers to Skeeter as "the black," he thinks, through the empathizing narrator, how funny it is that "everybody else has no trouble saying 'black' or hating the war. He must be defective" (198).

Harry's ideas about Vietnam will change next to nothing, and he is only slightly affected by Skeeter's views. At the end of the novel he tells Janice that he is too rational to know what Skeeter meant. But the very fact that he brings up this conversation with Janice and that he contradicts Stavros's rationalistic approach with Skeeter's mysticism, may indicate that he is now less certain as to what he should think about the Vietnam war. If he thinks it should come to an end is not clear. Although the issue had been resolved in earlier manuscripts, the final version of *Rabbit Redux* avoids the discussion at a very crucial moment in the novel, allowing for some ambiguity. Although Harry never expressed agreement with Skeeter's idea that "if the system, even if it works for most people, has to oppress some of the people, then the whole system should be destroyed" (216), he, no doubt, learned to tolerate blacks and hippies. The price he has to pay for allowing these people to interfere with his life is dear: his neighborhood relations move from indifference to open expressions of anger, his house ends up being burned down, Jill dies in the fire, and his son thinks of him as a coward. Harry's final gesture of helping Skeeter escape from the police, tells us how far—not very—he is willing to go to challenge the existing institutions. He seems to have regained the old Rabbit energies and, symbolically enough, ends up wearing his old highschool clothes found at his parent's home. Janice looks younger, too. Both seem to have rejuvenated significantly, yet their recovered youth has also an immature and adolescent association. Having no job—Linotyping became obsolete and was replaced by offset machines—having no home to move to, having grown tired of their "adventures," Harry and Janice are ready to begin life together again. They end up asleep in a motel, and the reader is asked if it is O.K.

As in *Rabbit, Run*, here too we have a hope for a new beginning. If the novel is read as an independent unit, we can regard the ending as a possibility for freedom—Harry's great chance to move away from the deadness of Brewer and on to healthier environments. But, there are also hints that the opposite may happen. Harry continues to act as a puritan, is still sexually afraid of Janice, preferring the abstraction of women to women themselves, and his final adolescent posture seems to be more a sign of regression or forceful adaptation to new circumstances rather than a clear understanding of what is happening. He still seems too small to live a free, inner-directed, independent life.

With the knowledge of the information given to us in *Rabbit is Rich*, the interpretation of *Rabbit Redux* becomes less ambiguous. Harry, we learn, again surrendered to the forces of the establishment, telling us that, even though exciting, the "adventures" with blacks and hippies have not changed him essentially. He will, among other things, live at the Springer's house for the next ten years, being pushed around like a puppet by Janice, her domineering mother, and her ghostly father. The liberation process, the movement from disease to health, which the novel can reveal in isolation, is lost when taken as part of the longer narrative. Harry's resistance to the establishment becomes, again, nothing but a momentary bravado without substance.

As we can see from this summary, Rabbit has changed, but only in the sense that the last ten years have made him even more outer-directed than he was in *Rabbit, Run*. Now, Rabbit, too, is a TV maniac and has no complaints. Nor does he complain about his job, even though he loses it because of technological innovations. The inner energy which once searched for the outstanding, for a first-rate life, is gone, and he has settled for mediocrity. His conservatism which was latent in the fifties has become open and aggressive. His need to win which in the fifties was more associated with a search for perfection, for an ideal, for self-improvement, in the sixties has become plain and pure war-mongerism.

But, certain things have changed so much in America, these last ten years, that Rabbit is forced to make room for some anti-establishment ideas. Blacks have gained unprecedented political power, hippies are questioning the materialism of the system, and students and intellectuals throughout the country are protesting the Vietnam war. Thus, along with the pride that comes with the technological development, with man landing on the moon, with heart transplants becoming more common, comes also the frustration of having a divided nation at war with itself and with the world. The uniformity of the fifties has fallen apart, and Harry who had always thought that the enemy was outside has come to learn that he is inside, and while he accuses blacks, and hippies, and "foreigners,"[3] he himself is being accused of being the enemy. The dominant forces of America are being challenged and the story which *Rabbit, Redux* tells, in a few words, is the story of this challenge. And because the novel is historically-oriented, we should look at history in order to throw light on its symbology.

Like *Rabbit, Run*, *Rabbit Redux* starts at a very precise day, month, and year, reminding us of Updike's concern with historicity. *Rabbit Redux* starts on July 16, 1969, Tuesday, at around five o'clock in the evening. The day is a day of discovery for America. America's Apolo 11 blasted off for a moon trip. Astronauts Neil Armstrong and Edwin Aldrin will, for the first time in history, walk on the moon. When the novel starts, we find Rabbit and his father going to a bar for a drink, after work. At the bar, the television is turned on, and "for the twentieth time that day the rocket blasts off, the numbers pouring backwards in tenths of seconds faster than the eye until zero is reached" (16). Everywhere Americans are hooked to the television set watching their "Columbus" discover a new America. But, the feat which unites Americans also seems to separate them from each other or, at least, it stresses the differences which exist between them. The workers at the bar, see "the lifting so slow it seems certain to tip, the swift diminishment into a retreating speck, a jiggling star" (16), but "they have not been lifted, they are left here" (16). Updike's suggestion, in the very first pages of the novel—that the common man should not expect much from this American "adventure"—foreshadows some of the problems Rabbit will have in his professional life, because of the technological innovations. It also shows the existing capital and labor conflicts, which never receive much foreground attention, but which Updike cannot help referring to at least.

The launching of Apolo 11 also shows, however, that all Americans feel proud of "these pretty boys in the sky right now" (20), because they all feel that they "have done [their] part" (20). The city of Brewer wastes no time in advertising itself. The article Rabbits typesets for the *Vat*, the newspaper he helps to print, reads as follows:

> When Brewerites this Sunday gaze up at the moon, it may look a little different to them.
> Why?
> Because there's going to be a little bit of Brewer on it.
> Zigzag Electronic Products Inc., of Seventh and Locust Streets, [...] city, revealed to VAT reporters this week that a crucial electronic switching sequence [...] was manufactured by them here (34).

Earl Angstrom, Harry's father, also points to the political side of this issue. Whereas people like President Richard Nixon send down to the masses "the manna of blessings" (20), trying to "hog the credit" (20), Rabbit's father feels that "it was the Democrats who put them there" (20), certainly referring to Kennedy's challenge, at the beginning of the decade, to overcome the Soviet supremacy in space exploration. His complaint that the "Republicans don't do a thing for the little man" (20), along with the narrator's comment that the common man has not been lifted with the Apolo 11, brings to light the text's intention of presenting America as a divided nation, showing at the same time the character's obvious anti-Republican stance.

The historic landing on the moon is also used by Updike to enhance the development of the conflicts between Rabbit and Janice. Early on Sunday morning on July 20, when the two astronauts are preparing to land on the moon, no matter what Rabbit thinks, it is associated with space imagery.[4] Thus, while weeding his lawn he sees "his hand with its ugly big moons on the fingernails" (83); while shopping for a present for his sick mother's birthday, which coincides with this historic day, Harry tells himself that "the pain of the world is a crater all these syrups and pills a thousandfold would fail to fill" (85); walking on the deserted sunday-afternoon streets, Rabbit asks: "Where is everybody? Is there life on earth?" (85); reflecting on his parents' home in Mount Judge, he thinks of it as being on "the dark half" (86); and the landing itself, the fact, the historic event, becomes confused with television animations and replays, and by the technical jargon used by the astronauts and Houston engineers. The babel that was created does not live up to the general expectations in the Angstroms home: Nelson falls asleep, Mr. Angstrom "is asleep in his chair, his breathing a distant sad sea" (92), and Rabbit's mind is so concerned with his own life now that Janice left him that when the video shows "electronic letters traveling sideways [spelling out] MAN IS ON THE MOON" (92), he produces a sentence which is a marvelous example of ambiguity at the service of art: "I don't know, Mom," he abruptly admits. "I know it's happened, but I don't feel anything yet" (93). Like the workers at the bar, he has not been lifted. Neil Armstrong had landed on the moon, Janice Angstrom had landed at her lover's apartment, and the two become confused in Harry's mind. Both, in their search for outer space, create emptiness, confusion, and anxiety in his inner space. Asking

his son whether he wants to go home, he is answered with the
astronauts' and technicians' jargon:

> "Negative, Pop." He drowsily grins at his own
> wit.
>   Rabbit extends the joke. "The time is twenty-one
> hours. We better rendezvous with our spacecraft"
> (92).

But the jocose mood soon vanishes when Harry thinks of his
home as an empty spacecraft, "a long empty box in the blackness
of Penn Villas" (92). The historic event, public in nature, has
become private and allegorical, and "the house is silent like
outer space" (80). But, because Rabbit himself is meant to be
read as an average American, a middle American, a representative of the "silent majority," a "solid citizen," his associations,
worries, verbal connections, jokes, and fears reacquire their
public nature. Thus, by using history and by endowing it with
allegorical meanings, sexual, political, and social, Updike manages to portray the inner-life of America during an unforgettable
year, month, week, day, moment of the country's life, showing
not only the event in its "neutrality," but how people reacted to
it, from the president to the high technology industry, from the
bus drivers to the printers, from adults to children.

Another historic circumstance that *Rabbit Redux* explores at
length is Senator Edward Kennedy's car accident on Saturday,
July 20, 1969. The use of this piece of history is not as rich alle-
gorically as the moon landing, but it shows, superbly, the varied
views that different characters have of their leaders. Whereas
Earl Angstrom uses the landing on the moon to denounce the
undeserved credit-hunting of the Nixon Administration, praising at the same time the Democrats for their great concern for
the "little man," Mr. Springer, Rabbit's father-in-law, uses the
Kennedy accident to point to the irresponsible behavior of "the
future President" (78), using the opportunity to slash not only
the Kennedy Administration but also the past Democratic Presidents, from Franklin Delano Roosevelt to Lyndon Johnson.

Updike's device of having a Republican reacting to the Kennedy incident allows him to counter-balance the previous

attacks on the Republicans. Updike's characters rather than his narrator bring up the controversy, creating a sense of neutrality in the political treatment of the incident and, especially, a sense of hopelessness in Rabbit's nationalistic mind. The country in which he believes so much seems to be under attack by all and sundry, and the different political preferences within his own family affirm that the leaders, regardless of party, are to blame.

Mr. Springer's revelation of the Kennedy incident is a perfect example of politically-oriented slanting. He does not report the incident, he evaluates and judges it according to his own political preferences. To start with, the incident is brought into the conversation at a moment when Rabbit makes his observation of how bad the situation of the country is:

> "Things go bad. Food goes bad, people go bad,
> maybe the whole country goes bad [...] I don't
> know. I don't know anything" (76)

Who is to blame? Mr. Springer wastes no time in bringing up the one-day old Ted Kennedy incident to find the answer. It is the incident which will give him the ammunition he needs to explain that the present predicament of the country is the Democrats' fault. Mr. Springer's talking out of the side of his mouth, "as if to shield Nelson, yet so distinctly the child can easily hear" (77) is also a way of making the incident sound as shameful as possible. With all this acting, one cannot expect an attempt at producing a description of what happened. Thus, Mr. Springer's report is heavily charged with judgments and hasty inferences:

> "Apparently, Harry [...] he dumped some girl from
> Pennsylvania into one of those Massachusetts riv-
> ers. Murder as plain as my face" (77).

Nelson's immediate question is not an attempt to find out what exactly happened. He does not want a description of the scene, either. Instead, Nelson asks, "Did they get him? Is he in jail, Grandpa" (77)? As we can see, his question implies an acceptance of his Grandfather's biased report and, consequently, he asks a question which allows Mr. Springer to proceed with his biased argument. The old man's answer, with its deliberately slanted way of looking at the incident, is obvious: "they'll never put a Kennedy in jail. Palms will be greased. Evidence will be suppressed" (77).

The implication is that Kennedys enjoy special privileges, because they sort of own the country or because they can even buy justice according to their needs. And if there are special privileges, how can we "call this a democracy" (77)? What would he call it? "I'd call it a police state run by the Kennedy's, is what I would call it" (77). What are the arguments? Mr. Springer goes again to history for help, showing how the wealthy Kennedy's have been trying "to buy the country since those Brahmins up in Boston snubbed old Joe. And then he put himself in league with Hitler when he was FDR's man in London. Now they've got the young widow to marry a rich Greek in case they run out of American money" (77). From Ted to Joe to FDR to John to Jacqueline to LBJ, it is all one smooth transition in Mr. Springer's mind. The premises of the syllogism are these: the Kennedy's are irresponsible; the Kennedy's are Democrats. Conclusion: The Democrats are irresponsible. He even offers a few examples to support his point: all major wars were started by the Democrats, FDR bailed his way out of Depression by finagling "the little Japanese into attacking Pearl Harbor" (78), and LBJ, just "to get the coloreds up into the economy, [went into Vietnam]. "That's why you have these wars, believe it or not, to bail the Democrats out of their crazy economics" (78).

As with the landing on the moon, the Ted Kennedy incident serves the purpose of helping Rabbit and the reader ponder over the state of American social and political life in 1969. Again, the picture the reader is presented is one of an America divided, distrusting her institutions, her police force, her judges, her political leaders. The same way the workers do not feel lifted by the blasting off of the Apolo 11, Rabbit is unable to enjoy the baseball game to which he goes with his father-in-law and his son. After hearing Mr. Springer's comments on the state of the country, Rabbit is too depressed to enjoy himself. But, the old man's speech, having visibly affected his feelings, has done nothing to change his mind. Although he is uneasily aware that "something has gone wrong with the country" (79), he feels that "America is still the only place" (79), reminding us of the boy of "First Person Singular." The feeling that Rabbit gets, i.e., that the country is extremely divided on most issues and that neither Democrats nor Republicans seem to be able to adequately manage the present affairs of the country, is also the reader's, forcing one to ask what is the way out.

The American presence in the Vietnam War was, perhaps, the greatest, dividing factor in the nation, and *Rabbit Redux*, in a very condensed way, faithfully reflects it. The Cold War had created a united front at home during the fifties, and dissent, because of the political intolerance of that "scoundrel time," as Lillian Hellman called it, was virtually invisible or unnoticed. By the end of the sixties, Vietnam was no longer only another manifestation of the Cold War policies, it was the Cold War transformed into an actual war. By the end of the decade, American involvement in Vietnam was such that Lyndon Johnson regarded it as impossible to fight the war with a disunited country. On March 31, 1968, the President decided not to seek reelection. Why not? Because:

> This country's ultimate strength lies in the unity of our people. There is division in the American house now. There is divisiveness among all of us tonight. And holding the trust that is mine, as President of all the people, I cannot disregard the peril to progress of the American people....With America's future under challenge right here at home...I do not believe that I should devote an hour or a day of my time to any personal partisan causes. Accordingly, I shall not seek, and will not accept, the nomination of my party for another term as president.[5]

The division that Johnson saw "in the American house" is also the division Updike portrays in *Rabbit Redux*. And the main foreign cause of this internal division was the Vietnam war. Johnson's exclusive dedication to the attempt to unite the country around this common cause — win the war and save South East Asia from communism — was a dismal failure. During the first Nixon Administration the American forces opposed to the war were still growing stronger.

Rabbit, as was pointed out earlier, is a nationalist who associates his nationalism with anti-communism, and therefore, brings the Truman/Eisenhower/Dulles version of McCarthyism into the sixties. For him those who oppose the war cannot be properly called Americans. He hates draft resisters, blacks, and "foreigners" like Stavros, yet he himself cannot properly convince himself that he is right about his posture.

One of the most remarkable discussions about the Vietnam War occurs in the Greek restaurant scene between Harry and Charlie, with some occasional interferences of Nelson and Janice. The discussion starts with the very fact that they are not in an American restaurant and Harry and his son do not know what to order, feeling lost, as if they were in a foreign country, which in a way is true, considering their habit of always eating at Burger Bliss whenever they go out. Thus, when Janice refers to them as "so American, they're helpless" (46), Stavros asks him about the flag decal he put on his car. Rabbit's nationalism is immediately ignited. Whereas Stavros argues that it is "somebody's flag" (46), trying to point out that it represents more a dominant group within the nation rather than the nation as a whole, Rabbit sees it as "our flag" (46), as opposed to other nations of the earth, especially China, which Rabbit, like the establishment, identifies as the new enemy. As with Lyndon Johnson, he cannot tolerate the division which right now exists in the American home, and he wants only to see "we" as opposed to "them," and it makes his blood boil when the government is being contradicted, again reminding us of the boy of "First Person Singular," who sees the President as mixed up with the flag and God, at the highest point of the hierarchichal ladder, and, therefore, as untouchable.

Stavros also makes it clear that what he means by "somebody's flag" is "the Pentagon playing cowboys and Indians all over the globe. That's what your little sticker means to me. It means screw the blacks and send the CIA into Greece" (47). It also means economic exploitation abroad, and stealing Jamaica's bauxite (51). Stavros, therefore, associates America with the dominant powers and with the profits corporations can make by controlling or taking over the natural resources of other countries.

Updike's decision to bring Greece into the discussion is remarkably appropriate to help Stavros, the son of a son of a Greek immigrant, not a foreigner as Rabbit wants him to be, make his point about the motives of American presence in Vietnam and throughout the world. It also reveals Updike's awareness about America's sponsorship and direct involvement in the anti-leftist crackdown in Greece in the forties and fifties when fourteen thousand people were rounded up and exiled without trial to island concentration camps, under the direct supervision of American Ambassador Lincoln MacVeagh, and under protest of the British. Noam Chomsky quotes American Ambassador Lincoln MacVeagh as justifying his actions saying that they "had to throw their net very wide to catch the right people."[6] Updike was probably also aware of the American backing of the neo-fascist Greek coup in 1967, backed by the United States and openly welcome by the Secretary of Commerce Maurice Stans, who was quoted in the *New York Times* as praising "the welcome that is given here to American companies and the sense of security the government of Greece is imparting to them."[7] By having a pleasant character like Stavros reacting to a narrow-minded and racist Rabbit, the reader is led to believe that Stavros's view of American business-oriented foreign policy is also Updike's.

Rabbit is incapable of this distinction. For him America is an abstraction hovering above all class and race distinctions, dominated by the white race, it is true, but that is what and how it should be, and anyone who refuses to pledge allegiance to that is betraying the country which has allowed him "to make a fat buck" (46). He tries to ridicule Stavros's argument that profits are at the root of American involvement in Vietnam. Why would America want their rice? For Uncle Ben? "The Uncle Ben Theory" (48) as Rabbit calls it, does not seem to work. Thus, Stavros tries another theory on Rabbit, probably also an allusion to the "Domino Theory," saying that it is not so much that America wants the Vietnamese rice, but that America does not "want them, [the Communists], to have it. Or the magnesium. Or the coastline. It's a mistaken power play. We've been playing chess with the Russians so long we didn't know we were off the board" (48).[8]

Rabbit is not convinced by the "power-play theory" either, although, almost at the end of the novel, he does tell his sister Mim that Vietnam has to be fought "to keep the other guy off balance, to keep your options, to keep a little space around you" (310). When we meet Harry, however, in July 1969, we meet a man who believes that "America is beyond power, it acts as in a dream, as a face of God" (49). With these God-like attributes, he sees it as a mission, a divine mission, to be involved throughout the globe. It is the only way of helping the ignorant millions to conquer their freedom and save them from the jaws of darkness. America is the liberator, America is sanity, America is light — the communists are the opposite. And because he believes this, he insists that he not only "went where [America] told [him], [he]'d still go where they told [him]" (49). Three months later, Rabbit does not sound so sure of himself any longer, yet he still believes that Vietnam is necessary, and he justifies it with a rhetoric reminiscent of the Cold War spirit of the fifties.

Harry's problem in the sixties, then, seems to lie largely in his not having outgrown the political notions which justified America's foreign policy in the fifties. He still believes that the Korean conflict was necessary, as he believes now that American involvement in Vietnam is necessary. Although anticommunism can most of the time be seen at the root of these wars, Rabbit also suggests that wars are naturally necessary. Thus, he personally does not see these wars only as anti-communist, a way of facing a threat against American freedom, security, and sovereignty, it is also because a war now and then is seen as a necessary episode in the life of a nation:

> "My opinion is, you have to fight a war now and
> then to show you're willing, and it doesn't much
> matter where it is. The trouble isn't this war, it's this
> country. We wouldn't fight in Korea now. Christ,
> we wouldn't fight Hitler now. This country is so
> zonked out on its own acid, sunk so deep in its own

fat and babble and filth, it would take H-bombs on
every city from Detroit to Atlanta to wake us up,
and even then, we'd probably think we'd just been
kissed" (50).

What Rabbit considers the American big sleep is, strangely
enough, the decade of protest. The fifties, the decade of national
uniformity, are over, but Rabbit still seems to be playing according to its rules. The government no longer has "carte blanche"
to pursue its aggressive international policies, and Rabbit sees it
as a personal loss—a crystal-clear indication of the outer-direct-
edness of his politics. Again, Rabbit is out-of-step with the forces
of change. In the fifties, he was looking toward the past trying
to affirm an individuality which was losing its preponderance in
American life; now, in the sixties, he is looking at the Korean
war—a war to which Mrs. Smith and Stavros, and Mim refer
derogatorily as "that Korean thing"—and at the power-fabri-
cated national cohesion of the fifties. In both novels, Rabbit,
despite his essential identification with the dominant forces,
seems to be at least one decade behind. The slowness of his
adaptation has definitely to do with his eminently reactionary
and conservative outlook. Rabbit sacralizes authorities, institutions, and laws, and as in *Rabbit, Run*, if he can help it, he will
never foul, and he will learn to play the game to perfection.
Once the rules are changed, the absolute breaks down, change
itself becomes intolerable, and personal confusion sets in.

Stavros seems to have perceived quite well that Rabbit's problem in the sixties has to do with his not having outgrown the
political notions which justified American foreign policy in the
fifties. His suggestion in the middle of his Cold War comments
that Johnson was just another belligerent Kennedy with "a bigger thumb on the button" (48) stresses the outdatedness of Rabbit's trigger-happy and anti-communist position. Vietnam
becomes a result of this policy of the fifties and early sixties, and
Rabbit, like Johnson, has remained insensitive to the growing
non-conformity of the new decade. In a way Rabbit's tragedy is
Johnson's tragedy a few years later. Rabbit's recalling of Johnson's offer to the Vietnamese is certainly no accident:

"Poor old LBJ, Jesus with tears in his eyes on
television, you must have heard him, he just about
offered to make North Vietnam the fifty-first fucking state of the Goddam Union if they'd just stop
throwing bombs. We're begging them to rig some
elections, any elections, and they'd rather throw
bombs" (47).

A comparison of Rabbit's description of Lyndon Johnson's
offer to the actual text of the President's speech leaves no doubt
about the influence of Johnson's ideas upon Rabbit.[9] Like Johnson, Rabbit, too, sees the American mission in the world as
impossible to be refused. The idea that the Vietnamese "aggres-
sors" might refuse a pax Americana can only be the result of
madness, blindness, an open defiance, a declaration of war. The
notion that the Vietnamese might be fighting a legitimate
national-liberation war, that they might be dissatisfied with foreign interference in their affairs, that they see themselves as
capable of guiding their own lives — these ideas never cross Rabbit's mind.

Johnson's crushing of a democratic revolution in the Dominican Republic in 1965 exemplifies well the reasoning behind the
American wars since the fifties. As evidence shows, Johnson's
justification of the American invasion was a fabrication and an
exaggeration of facts. The movement was not communist
inspired and was not carried out by Cuban and Soviet agents.
For the same reason that he failed to see the Vietnam War as a
struggle between Vietnamese, Johnson also refused to see the
Dominican Revolution as being fought between Dominicans.
Rabbit is a perfect reflection of this lack of political subtlety,
except that in his behavior we cannot identify possible deliberate
machinations. The world is divided in two — we and they, the
good and the bad guys, capitalists and communists, Soviets,
Chinese, and Cubans on one side, Americans on the other. Now
that large portions of Americans are refusing this simplistic view
of the world — as early as 1965, "twenty-five thousand anti-war
demonstrators marched in Washington"[10] — Rabbit and Johnson
are doing their best to keep the older model of the fifties and
early sixties intact.

As we have seen before, in the *Rabbit,Run* chapter, the American anti-communism of the fifties was quite successful in its purpose to keep inner-directedness under control while feeding the teleguiding corporate machine. The sixties started with a similar attempt. One only has to recall John Kennedy's inaugural address. As Robert Dallek points out, there is not one single issue in that address which could be described as purely national. Although in his first draft of the speech many such references existed, the final version was cleaned of those conflict-generating issues. Kennedy, like Johnson, was also keenly aware that America had to speak in unison to the rest of the world, and the sound should be produced by the president and echoed by the masses. Stavros's link between Kennedy and Johnson in their common attitude towards foreign affairs does not come out of the blue. It expresses the author's acute awareness of the major ideological constructs which guided American behavior with regards to Vietnam and other regions of the earth.

National unity, however, cannot be easily produced in a country with as much social, cultural, political, religious, and economic diversity as the United States. What had been good for the previous decades (World War II proved excellent to unite the country which was tearing apart after Roosevelt's ill-fated New Deal, as Mr. Springer tells us in *Rabbit Redux,* confirming what many commentators, e.g. Robert Bendiner and Michael Gold, had said before; Korea and other nationalist and socialist revolutions also proved excellent to unify the country, creating what is referred to in *Rabbit, Run* as the common view of the "class of 51") started proving unfeasible in the sixties. The movements for the liberation of the Negro, the anti-materialist, anti-capitalist Hippie movement, the sexual liberation of women — all these started posing legitimate questions which the establishment, along with Rabbit, had to answer. Updike dedicates a chapter of *Rabbit Redux* to each of these trends which cause division in the American home.

Updike's choice of a character like Skeeter as a symbol of the black resistance against racial and social discrimination at home is emblematic of the movement during the second half of the decade. By 1966, writes Robert Allen, "the traditional southern-based movement had largely ground to a halt and was in its death throes."[11] The Malcolm X anti-capitalist, anti-integration-ist, and revolutionary preachings started gaining more and more influence. After the assassination of Malcolm X, in 1965, Stokely Carmichael, the Black Panthers, and the SNCC (Student's Non-violent Coordinating Committee) tried to follow his thought and redefine black power. Updike's Skeeter becomes a representative type if seen in this context. Skeeter's militant anti-establishment attitudes are also essentially a disbelief in the possibility of jus-tice for blacks in a system that is eminently racist, and which, despite legal conquests by blacks, does not allow for the appli-cation of anti-segregationist laws. The denunciation of the sys-tem, the refusal to cooperate, and the determination to make use of violence as a means to achieve one's goals are all expres-sion of dissenting forces of the Civil Rights movement. Martin Luther King's discussion of the black power movement in his book *Where Do We Go from Here: Chaos or Community* (1967) con-firms Allen's version. Updike's exploration of this facet of the black movement becomes especially relevant because it repre-sents, ideologically at least, the greatest internal threat to the establishment ever. As Robert Allen puts it: "the mass mind of white America was gripped with fear and horror at the thought that blackness and power could be conjoined."[12] Rabbit belongs to this mass mind of white America, and as the empathizing narrator puts it, right after Rabbit decides to let Skeeter stay in his house for "a couple of days" (189), "he is terrified at having taken this man in. He will have to sleep with this man in the house. The tint of night. Skeeter will sneek to his side with a knife shining like the moon. He will get the gun as he has prom-ised [...] He is poison, he is murder, he is black" (189).

Although Rabbit had previously complained that there were blacks all over the place, on the buses, on television, on the streets — his racism becoming evident at every thought, uttered sentence, or encounter — his neighborhood had not yet faced the black anti-establishment militancy of Skeeter this closely. Skeeter's aggressiveness is such that both men had not talked for more than five minutes before everything Rabbit regards as sacred was challenged, vilipended, and profanated. Skeeter's first "greeting" words are "Hell, man, it's revolution, right?" (183) and he is quick to declare that his mission is to "undermine the state" (184). It soon becomes evident that Skeeter regards Rabbit as a representative of the white establishment and that the shower of insults at Rabbit's mother, who is described as a whore, at Rabbit's father, who is described as a queer, at Rabbit's God, who is described as "queerer than the Queen of Spades" (187), and at Rabbit's virility are actually directed at Skeeter's abstraction of the establishment which Rabbit impersonates. Compared to this outpour of insults, Stavros's previous criticisms become a child's complaint, and one cannot help observing how Stavros is integrated to the system when compared to Skeeter, who seems to be totally at its margin.

Skeeter's marginality certainly accounts for Updike's need to have him constantly remind the reader that Harry is the white American establishment. Discussion of political or racial issues between the two men is impossible without taking them as representatives of their races. They see each other as such, and we are asked to do the same. Roughly put, they are exactly antithetical: black versus white, slave versus slave owner, oppressor versus oppressed, establishment versus revolution.

When Skeeter first shows up at Rabbit's home, Rabbit asks him to turn himself in to the police, an idea which for Rabbit is perfectly reasonable because "this isn't the South" (185), but which for Skeeter is absolutely ridiculous and suicidal. For him "the South is everywhere" (185) and everywhere, even "way up in Detroit, they are shooting nigger boys like catfish in a barrel" (185). Thus, whereas for Skeeter there is no escape because all America is the same, i.e., unfair and cruel in its treatment of blacks, Rabbit has a blind faith in the institutions, prompting Skeeter's ridicule of his "white gentleman's concept of the police and their exemplary works" (185).

Skeeter's distrust of the white man's intention is such that when Rabbit decides to allow him to stay in his home, the only explanation he can find for Rabbit's decision is "a little tokenism

to wash [his] sins away" (189). Obviously, Skeeter's reasoning
identifies Rabbit not only with the existing establishment but
also with the past history of the country and with the white
man's policies towards blacks throughout this history. At this
point in their discussion, we have left the individuals, Skeeter
and Harry Angstrom, and moved toward a broader American
"cosmos" which they constitute. Skeeter's understanding is that
whatever the white man has done for the black man was done
"for selfish reasons" (189) and deserves no gratitude. Rabbit's
gesture of allowing him to stay becomes in Skeeter's mind a
reminder of all the times the negroes were promised things and
then betrayed. Being given something for nothing is a concept
Skeeter cannot understand as possible in a black-white relationship, and he somehow wonders what the price will be this time
when the white man allows him under the same roof, behaving
like "a fucking Good Samaritan...[taking] in these orphans.
Black, white...irregardless of color or creed...free eats...[like]
the fucking Statue of Liberty" (311). This feeling finds some
justification in the novel, for Harry can only do what he did
having asserted his authority through the use of physical violence, making it very clear whose the house is and who has the
upper hand. Later in the novel Mim tells Rabbit that she, too,
has learned to pay for anything she gets "because anything free
has a rattlesnake under it" (312), as if to confirm that Skeeter's
fears were perfectly justified.

Skeeter's use of the Civil War to help him make his point about
the white man's exploitation of the negro is in the same frame of
mind and helps us understand his distrust and his abstraction
of Rabbit as the white establishment:

> "Lincoln got this war, right, and fought it for a
> bunch of wrong reasons—what's so sacred about a
> **Union,** just a power trust, right?—and for another
> wrong reason freed the slaves, and it was done.
> God bless America , right? So here I begin to get
> mad" (204).

Skeeter's anger has to do with the way he reads this period of
history. The slaves were freed for the wrong reasons, i.e., for

economic rather than humanitarian reasons. Profit was the determinant factor, not justice. After Lincoln's decision, "you had these four million freed slaves without property or jobs in this economy dead on its feet thinking the halleluiah days had come, Green pastures, right? Forty acres and a mule, right?" (205).[13] The end result of Lincoln's decision, as Skeeter sees it, was that "the South got slavery back at half the price, it got control of the Congress by counting the black votes that couldn't be cast, the North got the cotton money it needed for capital, and everybody got the fun of shitting on the black man and then holding their noses" (207). Updike's later study of the forces at the root of the Civil War in *Buchanan Dying* (1974), along with the continued virtual slavery of blacks until the sixties, confirms Skeeter's interpretation and somehow justifies his bitterness and hatred.

When asked if he agrees with Skeeter's interpretation of the history of the Civil War, Rabbit says that he believes "all of it" (207). This admission, however, is probably more the result of Rabbit's ignorance on the issue than a genuine belief, for it contradicts other comments of his that claim, more consistently with his frame of mind, that Skeeter's reading of history seems to be that America's only purpose has been to exploit and torture Negroes. Nevertheless, Rabbit's statement that he believes in the truth of what Skeeter tells him about the Civil War prompts Skeeter to identify Rabbit, even more clearly than before, with the traitors of the black race:

> "What I want to say to you, what I want to make ever so clear, Chuck, is you had that chance. You could have gone some better road, right? You took that greedy turn, right? You sold us out, right? [...] and you didn't lift us up, we held our hands, man, we were like faithful dogs waiting for that bone, but you gave us a kick, you put us down, you put us down" (207).

When Skeeter says "you" he means both "Harry" and "America." Reading the text with this substitution in mind makes the perception of Rabbit as a symbol of the establishment unmistakably clear. Thus, when Skeeter tells Rabbit that "you really had it here, you had it all, you took that greedy mucky road, man, you made yourself the asshole of the planet" (207), we have no doubt whatsoever that he is not really talking to Rabbit, he is talking to the country, to America.

What should be remembered here is that Skeeter, while he is able to identify Rabbit with middle America, with the establishment, and with America's dominant text, he is also able to portray himself as marginal to that text. He becomes, in Derridian language, the white of the page. This is something Stavros cannot do, despite his disagreements with the politics of "the silent majority." Like the black integrationists, Stavros suggests that America's problems are mistakes which can be remedied with appropriate political reforms. Vietnam is a mistake, the treatment of blacks is a mistake. Both can be corrected and avoided in the future.

Updike's choice of a character like Skeeter allows him to go beyond the integrationist and reformist views. For Skeeter, America cannot be reformed—it has to be destroyed. America is inherently wicked and will continue to be so. Vietnam and slavery, in this light, are not mistakes. They are what America, by its very nature, has to be. Thus, when Rabbit asks Skeeter— "is our being in Vietnam wrong?" (231)—Skeeter refuses to openly consider the American presence in terms of right or wrong. He feels beyond that question; in fact, he feels it is the wrong question to ask:

> "Wrong? Man, how can it be wrong when that's the way it is? These poor Benighted States just being themselves, right? Can't stop bein' yourself, somebody has to do it for you, right? Nobody that big around. [...] I'm not one of these white lib-er-als [...] think Vietnam some sort of mistake we can fix it once we get the cave men out of office, it is **no** mistake, right, any President comes along falls in love with it [...] Nam the spot where our heavenly essence is pustulating. Man don't like Vietnam, he don't like America" (232).

This passage allows us to place Skeeter very clearly on the other extreme of the ideological spectrum, a spectrum which has at its right Rabbit (present more as scene upon which the other forces act) followed by Mr. springer, Mr. Angstrom, with Stavros and Janice at the center, and with Jill, Mim, and Nelson leaning toward the left but placed at a considerable distance from the world of Skeeter. Rabbit, because he operates more as a scene upon which these forces act rather than as an agent, is always somehow a center of dispute. What the quotation above also tells us is that Skeeter does not believe that the American foreign policy can be corrected — it has to be stopped by somebody else, a bigger, stronger power, a power whose existence, like Mim, he doubts. Similarly, he does not believe that the racial segregation can be amended; it, too, has to be destroyed by a greater power. Thus, there is no way of talking sense into politicians and presidents — the only solution is to force fundamental changes in the structure of the system, so that its very **nature** is changed, so that it ceases to be what it is.

That racism and Vietnam are so intricately connected in *Rabbit Redux* is certainly no accident at all. The books Skeeter brings into Rabbit's house ("The Selected Writings of W. E. B. DuBois, The Wretched of the Earth, Soul on Ice, The Life and Time of Frederick Douglas, others, history, Marx, economics, stuff that makes Rabbit feel sick" (201)) are indications enough that Skeeter has learned to see the racial issue as part of a broader economic system. Thus, racism and neo-colonialism are regarded as part of the same problem, capitalism. When one hears Skeeter denouncing the savagery of American capitalism, especially after the Civil War, when as he puts it the South decided to "screw the black labor" and the North, as part of the agreement, decided to exploit the "immigrant honky and idiot labor" (206), we cannot help thinking of Malcolm X (Skeeter actually says that his surname is 42 X) and Stokely Carmichael and their notion that imperialism and neo-colonialism as practiced by America in other parts of the world is part of the same internal colonialism practiced against blacks and other workers at home. Malcolm X's dedicated solidarity with the exploited peoples of the third world stems from a belief that blacks in America are part of the same third world, and that, therefore, their enemy is the same, capitalism.[14] Like Skeeter, Malcolm X could not see any possibility in reforming and integrating. For him it was absurd to try to integrate blacks into a decadent society. George Breitman, in his book *The Last Year of Malcolm X* quotes Malcolm as saying:

> The system in this country cannot produce freedom
> for an Afro-American. It is impossible for this sys-
> tem, this economic system, this social system, this
> system, period. It's impossible for this system, as it
> stands, to produce freedom right now for the black
> man in this country.[15]

Malcolm went even further in his connection of capitalism and racism. Robert Allen points out that in answer to a question from an audience, Malcolm once replied that "it's impossible for a white person to believe in capitalism and not believe in racism. You can't have capitalism without racism."[16] Breitman also quotes Malcolm as saying that it is impossible to operate a capitalistic system "unless you are vulturistic; you have to have someone else's blood to suck to be a capitalist. You show me a capitalist, I'll show you a bloodsucker..."[17] Like Skeeter, Malcolm sees America's treatment of blacks and workers as a natural capitalistic policy of exploitation. Loving America, therefore, becomes synonymous to loving capitalism and what it does at home and abroad. This explains why Skeeter concludes that you cannot love America and not love Vietnam, and why Malcolm made many attempts to internationalize the struggle of American blacks. During his trips around Africa, for example, he tried with little success to have the African nations denounce America's disrespect for human rights in the United Nations and the World Court. Unlike Rabbit, Skeeter and Malcolm do not see a classless America, neutrally hovering above class interests. They see America as a powerful corporation, an association of capital, so powerful that it can influence and interfere with almost every aspect of life in the United States and in many parts of the world.

If the class struggle is prior to the racial struggle, however, one has to ask why Rabbit and Skeeter represent exact opposite poles of the ideological spectrum. Rabbit is a worker and should, therefore, be able to express solidarity for the black struggle, if indeed it is a struggle of labor against capital. Instead, as we have seen, he is a vicious racist, and does not see any reason why he should identify with blacks, a behavior which is somewhat repressed by the end of the novel but which never disappears.

More than one explanation may be necessary here. First, one has to recall that although Harry identifies himself and is identified by others with the establishment, he is not a subject but an object of history, i.e., his conservatism is not his own, his ideology is not his own, and his life, to a large extent, is not his own. What makes Jill so angry at one point is that Rabbit does not seem to perceive that he is being used by the system (185) and that he is a victim even though the establishment describes him as a perfectly "solid citizen" (286). Stavros's description a little earlier makes Rabbit's teleguidedness even clearer. He describes Rabbit as "a normal product...a typical good-hearted imperialist racist" (49). A product, not a producer. This characterization adds to Skeeter's view of Rabbit as the establishment, but whereas Skeeter, full of hatred and resentment, is more interested in pointing out Rabbit's identification with the dominant ideology and its dreadful consequences, Stavros, by making the point that Rabbit's life is teleguided, feels in greater need to understand and forgive. Stavros, the worker, does have sympathy for blacks, but, then, Stavros, the white worker, unlike Rabbit, also understands that imperialist forces act as much upon "little yellow people" in Vietnam as they act upon blacks and whites at home. This bit of understanding is denied to Rabbit.

But, the identification with the establishment may not be the whole explanation for Rabbit's incapacity to identify with the struggle of blacks. Updike's text also reflects Malcolm X's and Stokely Carmichael's view of white workers' solidarity toward the Negro cause, and this is where another explanation may reside. Carmichael wrote in the mid-sixties that he hoped "to see, eventually, a coalition between poor blacks and poor whites. Poor whites everywhere are becoming more hostile — not less — partly because they see the nation's attention focused on black poverty and nobody coming to them."[18] While commenting on Carmichael's view of white workers, Robert Allen observed that "he certainly recognized [that] the white industrial workers—long the hope of the white left—seeing their own security threatened, can now be counted among the most vicious racists in the country."[19] Rabbit, although not an industrial worker, is a typical representative of this attitude and, as if to retrospectively support Carmichael's view, Updike has Rabbit lose his job—a job he could have kept were it not for his black co-workers. Having achieved a level of organization which gave blacks a significant bargaining power, with "all do-good outfits" on their side, the white bosses seem reluctant or even fearful to fire them. Pajasek's observation to Rabbit, while telling him that he will have to leave because "they've decided up top to make Verity an offset plant" (296), deserves to be quoted because it illustrates so well the concerns of Carmichael and Malcolm X about the difficulties which a black-white alliance would face:

> "We can keep a few men on, retrain them to the computer tape, we've worked the deal out with the union, but this is a sacrifice, Harry, from the management point of view. I'm afraid you're far down the list. Nothing to do with your personal life, understand me—strictly seniority. Your Dad's secure, and Buchanan, [who is black], Christ, let him go we'd have every do-good outfit in the city on our necks, it's not the way I'd do things. If they'd come to me I would have told them, that man is half-soused from eleven o'clock on every morning, they're all like that, I'd just as soon have a moron with mittens on as long as he was white" (297).

That Rabbit does not express any resentment toward Buchanan, could lead us to believe that Rabbit outgrew his racism and is now ready to even sacrifice his job for a black man's happiness. As Updike's text indicates, however, there is little Harry, Pajasek, or white America can do. The new predicament is more the result of political space which has been conquered by blacks than a result of a fundamental change in their attitude towards blacks. His racist manifestations continue as rampant as before. Rabbit's lies about Skeeter at the police station show that Skeeter "has become in his backwards vision little more substantial than a shadow behind a chair" (300). Instead of a commitment, Skeeter has been transformed into a ghost—a ghost which will haunt him for the next ten years, as *Rabbit is Rich* tells us, showing that, although aware, he has never come to terms with the negro demands and presence. Finally, by making Pajasek, Mr. Angstrom, and Rabbit similar in their prejudices towards blacks, Updike has tipped the scale toward the same fears and prejudices which Carmichael saw as responsible for making a white-black alliance unfeasible and unlikely.

The references to Robert Williams's return to America from China, after many years in exile, show that Skeeter's presence in the book is also a reminder that many blacks saw with disbelief the power of the non-violent protests which had started a decade earlier. Robert Williams, one should remember, had already in the late fifties, "organized a chapter of the National Rifle Association among blacks in Monroe, North Carolina" and had his armed men rescue some peaceful demonstrators who were being mercilessly beaten by the police, during a six-day protest at a courthouse in Monroe. The knowledge of this information makes the piece of news the characters listen to at Rabbit's house much more meaningful. First, we understand how the establishment has managed to silence Williams by forcing him into exile as it somehow had managed to silence other leaders like Malcolm X, Eldrige Cleaver, and Martin Luther King. Second, we also understand that Skeeter is not a mirror-image of one specific historic character, but that instead he is more a distortion than an average, formed by the agglutination of various forces of the black movement, having a little of all of them, and not any longer capable of totally identifying himself with any of them.

Rabbit's ignorance about Robert Williams again is indicative of his borrowed ideology, for it shows that the establishment's propaganda system has been effective in silencing a voice which had been telling the world about the abuses of black people's rights in America. When his thirteen-year old son mentions that Williams is back in the country, Rabbit is forced to ask "who the hell is Robert Williams?" — to which Skeeter has a prompt reply: "he's a man going to fry your ass. You and Nixon's, right?" (200).

Skeeter, strangely enough, despite the reader's tendency to think of him as a member of the Black Panthers Party, refuses to acknowledge his kinship with Bobby Seale, on the grounds that Seale is an "establishment nigger" (241). Although Rabbit calls Skeeter's observation ridiculous for he sees him as being as "full of hate" (241) as the Black Panthers, Skeeter's refusal to recognize any connection with the Black Panthers may be interpreted as a foreshadowing of future political alliances which brought the group closer to the system's ways. The Chicago eight trials referred to in the TV news broadcast and the Oakland assembly organized by the Panthers, with a 90% white public participating, perhaps shows why Skeeter considers them, already in 1969, a lost case, false prophets. His turn to mysticism may well be taken as an expression of his sense of impotence in face of a Black Panther movement whose leader "has John Kennel Badbreath and Leonard Birdbrain giving him fund-raising cocktail parties" (241). Through Skeeter, Updike seems to have had, fifteen years ago, a glimpse of what would indeed happen to many representatives of the movement. Who could have fifteen years ago told that in 1986, Eldrige Cleaver, the famous revolutionary of the sixties, would be an active member of the GOP? Or that the famous leader of the Panthers would be writing…cook books. Only an outsider, a luminary like Updike's Skeeter.

Jill, too, is a representative type of the sixties — the hippies. Jill is a white self-marginalized member of the upper-middle class and because of her physical features has been identified by Kathleen Lathrop as a Patricia Hearst type. She can enjoy the material wealth of her country and of her family, but sees herself as part of a system which is petty, moralistic, repressive, narrowminded, materialistic, greedy, sexually prudish, and violent.

These contentions she has with the system led her to abandon her family, which had already been broken up by divorce, and to join the anti-Vietnam war movement, the black struggle, and the drug cult. It is not surprising, therefore, that the reader and

Rabbit find her among blacks, in a fearful and fragile alliance with an anti-Vietnam, anti-establishment black figure like Skeeter. Like Skeeter, Jill thinks "the system is rotten...and that the laws are written to protect a tiny elite" (185). Although she admits that she comes from among "people who own boats in Stonington," she feels proud that she "ran away from it...reject[ed] it and [can] shit on it" (185). In one word, Jill feels proud she is not like Rabbit, i.e., used by the system. Her analysis of Rabbit becomes a powerful ponderation on the nature of the life of "middle" America of the decade. And it is this reflection which makes Jill historically representative and, ipso facto, a necessary color in the ideological rainbow of *Rabbit Redux*.

Jill is very quick to perceive the outer-directed nature of Rabbit's life. She sees him as a representative of the establishment, but not as a maker of policies with national expression; she views him as an object teleguided and manipulated by corporate America. She sees Harry's life as lacking "reflective content...all instinct" (203), as extremely pragmatical, always ready to aim his action at an immediate utilitarian purpose, without ever taking the time to think about the meaning of the purpose which absorbs his energies. Jill's discourse deserves to be at least partly quoted, especially because of its almost unnoticeable transformation of Rabbit into a representative of the middle American man:

> "It's wrong," Jill goes on gently, "when you say Americans are exploiters, to forget that the first things they exploit are themselves. You...you've never given yourself a chance to think, except on techniques, basketball and printing, that served a self-exploitative purpose. You carry and old God with you, and an angry old patriotism. And now an old wife....You accept these things as sacred not out of love or faith but fear; your thought is frozen because the first moment when your instincts failed, you raced to the conclusion that everything is nothing, that zero is the real answer. That is what we Americans think, it's win or lose, all or nothing, kill or die, because we have never created the leisure in which to take thought. But now, you see,

> we must, because action is no longer enough,
> action without thought is violence. As we see in
> Vietnam" (203).

Jill's discourse reveals the ambiguity of her position and helps us understand why she has at the same time an "affair" with a representative of the establishment and with its most violent antagonist. Jill is torn between her vision of a different America, and her fear that it might change too much. She hates what Rabbit stands for, "the enemy's uniform, athlete and soldier" (157), yet it is in his arms that she finds comfort and safety after every interaction with Skeeter. The black militant, whom she brought into Rabbit's house, begging Rabbit to let him stay, frightens her so much that she soon pleads with Rabbit to get him out of the house, for "he's no good for me, no good for any of us" (208). The Jill/Skeeter alliance seems to rest more on the opposition to the establishment and on the escape from it through drugs than on a common goal or idealization of society.

Jill's ambiguity can also be seen in her shifting of perspective when talking about America. First, America is "they" then it is "you," and it ends being "we." In other words, first Jill perceives America as belonging to forces which exploit not only the world but other Americans as well; second, Jill identifies America with the Rabbits of the country, i.e., the middle Americans who reflect the exploitative forces and help to support them but which are different from them in that they are reproductions rather than originals; and, finally, Jill identifies herself with Americans, making herself somehow a creator of the present status quo and implying that she can recreate it.

It is at this point that Jill becomes very different from Skeeter, who, having his roots in the most oppressed of classes and races, cannot see himself or his race as subjects of history. Only now is he determined to alter that, but what is past is identified with those who held the bridles of the horses of history, the white race. Thus, although Skeeter can distinguish the "you" from the "they" the same way Jill does, he cannot use a "we." The first person plural pronoun would express an impossible identification with the white establishment, with which he feels no affinity whatsoever. Updike's changes in MS # 1020 confirms that this great marginalization of Skeeter was intentional.[20]

Jill's self-marginalization also allows her to realize that unless one thinks in terms which are not the system's, all one can do is reproduce the system, i.e., all one can do is think the way Rabbit does — in terms of techniques, basketball, and printing. Rabbit's mind is enslaved by the search of consistency with existing dominant behavior. It can never envision the possibility of questioning the collective assumptions. In *Rabbit Run* Rabbit understood only that he had to train himself to perfection in order to be a winner in the system; in *Rabbit Redux* his identification with the system is such that he can only think in terms of techniques to preserve and expand its power. His attitudes toward the Vietnam war, the hippies, and the black movement are, indeed, as Janice puts it, expression of his fear of seeing the "old-fashioned life [with its] old fashioned reasons" (54) crumbling right in front of him.

Jill's presence in the novel, then, is an attempt to convey the reality of the ideological spectrum of the sixties. Through Jill we discover other facets of Rabbit's establishment-oriented perspective, facets which other characters had referred to, but which Jill manages to verbalize with impressive clarity. Rabbit's anti-intellectual posture, his Skinnerian responses to complex political issues, his false moralism — all these are illuminated anew through Jill's portrayal of him as the middle American. But, as we can see from her fears of Skeeter's radicalism, she is situated way to the right of Skeeter. The fact that she refuses to cooperate with the system, however, places her to the left of Stavros, thus adding a new shade of color to the ideological spectrum.

It would be impossible to study *Rabbit Redux* without some reference to Mim, Harry's sister, who is a prostitute. Mim returns home for a short visit after Rabbit's ill-fated adventures with Jill and Skeeter. Now that Rabbit's home has been burned down, he and Nelson are living with his parents. Their meeting with Mim adds interesting insights on the behavior, especially sexual behavior, of the average American. Although Mim's short section does not contain topical events of the sixties, it helps to convey and reflect upon the sexual mood of the decade as it has been experienced by the major characters of the novel.

Mim is basically an intelligent and unscrupulous individualist, committed to no cause except herself, determined to live her own life. She makes a living selling herself to men and has developed special techniques to "milk people" without getting bored with them. By never going to bed with her lovers more than three times, she has managed to remain attractive to all of them. According to her, these are survival techniques — "rules for living in the desert" (312). Yet, because she rarely develops profound long-lasting relations, she conveys to the reader the feeling that the brother she finds so naive and her parents who are almost dead are still the only people she truly cares for. They are worth visiting; they seem worth "saving."

It is because of the ambiguity of this philosophy of hers that Rabbit's tragedy of having "lost" his wife to a lover becomes somewhat ludicrous. Knowing that Janice has an affair, she decides to check how good a lover Stavros is. Later, she tells Harry that Stavros is nothing special and that Janice will return to him. Indeed, Harry and Janice are reunited and, as husband and wife, decide to start their lives anew. Mim's reification of sexual experience, hints of which we have a decade earlier in *Rabbit, Run*, manages to successfully break the icons of sexuality while pointing to more meaningful human relationships in a period of search for female independence and sexual crisis.

But Rabbit has not changed significantly. Sexually, he still behaves prudishly, ashamed to enter a motel with his wife. When talking about his avoidance of Peggy Fosnacht he confesses to Janice that "all this fucking, everybody fucking...it just made [him] too sad. It's what makes everything so hard to run" (344). Besides, women seem to threaten him even more now that they have made sex such a commonplace thing. At the beginning of the novel, we find a Rabbit who "had fled [Janice's] cunt as a tiger's mouth" (33); by the time the novel ends, we find a Rabbit who somehow seems to have reverted to his adolescence. He wears his old highschool clothes and masturbates, finding the image of women more attractive and appealing than

women of flesh and bone and mind. All in all, Mim's presence
in the novel seems to be suggesting that the sixties have exposed
Rabbit and America to a number of very rich experiences, and,
although America has learned to marginally tolerate behaviors
which in the uniformity of the fifties were unacceptable, very
little has been absorbed into his heart and into the heart of the
establishment. Skeeter's radical political views, Jill's anti-mater-
ialistic outlook, Janice's extra-marital affairs, Peggy's divorce,
Mim's promiscuity and her ridicule of Lincoln's "sacredness of
the Union"—all act upon Rabbit in some ways, as he receives
them in his home, but, like middle America, Rabbit remains
fundamentally unchanged. Once these experiences of his have
been filtered through his pro-establishment mind frame, he
absorbs their secondary elements and distorts their revolutionary nature, making them part of the establishment. Thus, the
little and great tragedies of the decade are easily transformed
into triumphs, new energy, oil for the rusty engine. Rabbit will
"run" for another decade, reenergized, but his "mind" and his
"heart" still hold the same old concepts and feelings, although,
perhaps, they are a little more confused. The "crisis of confidence" which Paul Gray has identified in *Rabbit is Rich* has
started to show its first signs. Rabbit tells Mim that he has
"learned "that the country isn't perfect," but the empathising
narrator cannot help telling us that "even as he says this he
realizes he doesn't believe it, even more than he believes at heart
that he will die" (312). The search for Eden in the sixties may
indeed have become more political and secularized, as Morris
Dickstein claims, but not for Harry. The halo of established
authority has not been removed from his eyeballs. For middle
America, authority remains as sacred as ever. Little wonder,
then, that in the seventies we find Rabbit even more deeply
entrenched in the establishment. The victim will become a beneficiary; in the seventies the "solid citizen" is rich.

Notes

[1] John Updike, *Rabbit Redux* (New York: Fawcett Crest, 1961) 14. (All further references to this novel are cited parenthetically in the text).

[2] John Updike, *Assorted Prose* (New York: Alfred A. Knopf, 1974) 106.

[3] In Manuscript 1020, Updike had very explicitly given Rabbit a Swedish origin. There the Angstroms are described as being "Swedish by blood way back yet nevertheless because of it just missed fitting in." This whole line was crossed out. Had it stayed in, Rabbit would have had even less reason to call Stavros, a third-generation Greek immigrant, a "foreigner."

[4] An interesting study on the moon imagery in *Rabbit Redux*, which corroborates my argument, is Charles Berryman's article "The Education of Harry Angstrom: Rabbit and the Moon," published in *The Literary Review*, 27.1 (Fall 1983): 117-126.

[5] In Robert Dallek, *The American Style of Foreign Policy — Cultural Politics and Foreign Affairs* (New York and Scaborough, Ontario: A Mentor Book, 1983) 222.

[6] In Noam Chomsky, *Toward a New Cold War — Essays on the Current Crisis and How We Got There* (New York: Pantheon Books, 1982) 199.

[7] *The New York Times* 24 April 1971.

[8] Stavros's words gain natural credibility because of the Cold War spirit it recalls. This becomes especially so if one remembers this 1953 declaration of President Eisenhower: "If we lost Indochina and the Malay peninsula, the tin and tungsten we so greatly value from that area would cease coming...Finally, if we lost all that, how would the free world hold the rich empire of Indonesia? — the prodigious supplies of rubber and rice — the areas of Thailand and East Pakistan? So when the United States votes $400,000,000 to help [the French in] that war, we are not voting a give-away program. We are voting for the cheapest way we can to prevent the occurrence of something that would be of a most terrible significance to the U.S.A., our security, our power and ability to get certain things we need from the riches of the Indonesian territory and from Southeast Asia" (In Robert Allen, *Black Awakening in Capitalist America — An Analytic History* (Garden City, New York: Anchor Books, 1970) 44).

[9] Rabbit's reference is certainly to Lyndon Johnson's offer of a pax Americana to the Vietnamese made on April 7, 1965 in a speech delivered at Johns Hopkins University. The following excerpt of his speech shows no doubt the source of Rabbit's reactions: "For what do the people in North Vietnam want? They want what their neighbors also desire — food for their hunger, health for their bodies, a chance to learn, progress for their country, and an end to the bondage of material misery. And they would find all of these things are more readily in peaceful association with others than in the endless course of battle...For our part I will ask the Congress to join in a billion-dollar American investment as soon as it is under way...The Vast Mekong River can provide food and water and power on a scale to dwarf even our own TVA...The wonder of medicine can be spread through villages where thousands die every year from lack of care...I also intend to expand and speed up a program to make available our farm surplus to assist in feeding and clothing the needy in Asia...But we cannot and must not wait for peace to begin this job."

¹⁰ After the murder of SNCC worker Sammy Younge, Jr., in Alabama, when he tried to use a white restroom, the SNCC issued a statement opposing the Vietnam War, supporting draft resisters, and denouncing the abuse of civil rights at home. Part of the text read as follows: "We are in sympathy with an support the men in this country who are unwilling to respond to the military draft which would compel them to contribute their lives to U.S. aggression in the name of the "freedom" we find so false in this country." In Robert Allen, *Black Awakening in Capitalist America — An Analytic History.* (Garden City, New York: Anchor Books, 1970), 46.

¹¹ Ibid. p. 23.

¹² Ibid. p. 22.

¹³ Ibid p. 85. Item number 3 of the Black Panther's program also refers to the compensations promised to the black man. It reads as follows: "We want an end to the robbery by the white man of our black community. We believe that this racist government has robbed us and now we are demanding the overdue debt of forty acres and two mules. Forty acres and two mules was promised one hundred years ago as a restitution for slave labor and mass murder of black people. We will accept the payment in currency which will be distributed to our many communities..."

¹⁴ This is how Stokely Carmichael addressed a meeting of Latin American revolutionaries in Cuba in 1967: "We greet you as comrades because it becomes clear to us each day that we share with you a common struggle; we have a common enemy. Our enemy is white Western imperialist society. Our struggle is to overthrow this system which feeds itself and expands itself through the economic and cultural exploitation of non-white, non-Western peoples — the THIRD WORLD. Our people [the black people] are a colony within the United States; you are colonies outside the United States. It is more than a figure of speech to say that the black communities in America are the victims of white imperialism and colonial exploitation. This is in practical economic and political terms true." Ibid. pp. 6-7.

In March 1968 Eldrige Cleaver made a speech in California, along the very same lines: "We start with the basic definition: that black people in America are a colonized people in every sense of the term and that white America is an organized imperialist force holding black people in colonial bondage..." Ibid. p. 264.

¹⁵ In George Breitman, *The Last Year of Malcolm X* (New York: Merit, 1967) 33.

¹⁶ In Robert Allen, *Black Awakening in Capitalist America — an Analytic History* (Garden City, New York: Anchor Books, 1970) 32.

¹⁷ Ibid. pp. 35-36.

¹⁸ Ibid. p. 54.

¹⁹ Ibid. p. 55.

²⁰ In MS 1020, Skeeter tells Rabbit that he lost his wallet: "all my credit cards in it, NAACP membership,..." The excision is Updike's realization that Skeeter could not belong to this integrationist organization while at the same time preaching from an extremely marginal position. His revision is an expression of Updike's great care with the authenticity and consistency of his text. Without the alteration, Skeeter would have become associated with a particular label

without an adequate correspondence. The excision of "credit cards" retains at a socio-economic level the same kind of marginality we see in the political Skeeter. Again, it would be somewhat inconsistent of him to join the credit system of his arch-enemies. If Skeeter did have credit cards, they would have had to be stolen.

Chapter 4

The Hostage of Fortune

"True enough, there is this interest in the past,
but in a way the past is all we have. The present is
very thin, it's less than a second wide, and the
future doesn't exist"

(Picked-Up Pieces).

In *Rabbit is Rich* Rabbit **is** rich. He co-owns "Springer Motors, one of the two Toyota agencies in the Brewer area,"[1] and Toyotas are selling as they never sold before. Because of the international oil crisis, the cars actually sell themselves, and Rabbit has now more money in the bank than he could have ever dreamed of. He speculates with gold and silver, and, month after month, his wealth increases. His rich friends at the club—where Janice spends her afternoons playing tennis and sunbathing, and where he plays golf on weekends, "to feed the inner man" (240)—unknowingly act as his economic advisors. Rabbit also reads the papers, listens to the radio, watches TV, and, especially, gobbles up *Consumer Reports,* his new bible. In other words, Rabbit has finally achieved economic success; he is the employer, the boss, the proprietor, capital. And all thanks to the Arabs and their oil embargo and to the oil price increases. And also thanks to Toyota, the company which managed to produce the most economical car in the world, replacing the giant "gas-hogs" of the previous decades. And, because Rabbit happened to be at the right place at the right time, the "external circumstances" made him rich. A premium paid by the establishment for his years of loyalty to the system? Probably not even that; just a plain coincidence, an accident of history, a specific scenic arrangement.

But, how happy is Rabbit with his new life, living under the pushy mother-in-law he always detested and working side by side with his wife's former lover, now his best friend? When he thinks about it, which is not very frequently, he wonders what he has done "with this life of his more than half over. He was a good boy to his mother and then a good boy to the crowds at the basketball games, a good boy to Tothero, his old coach, who saw in Rabbit something special [...] What does he know? He never reads a book, just the newspaper to have something to say to people, and then mostly human interest stories, like where the Shah is heading next and how sick he really is, and that Baltimore doctor. He loves nature, though he can name almost nothing in it...he loves money, though he doesn't understand how it flows to him or how it leaks away...He used to love screwing, though more and more he's willing just to think about it and let the younger people mess with it...He tries to picture what will turn him on, and he's running out of pictures..." (129). Thus, although Rabbit is enjoying economic independence, he still seems troubled by the emptiness of his life, by its lack of excitement and interest, and by his incapacity to understand what the forces are which determine it. He lives daily life with a strict pragmatic approach, trying to serve his business as much as possible. And, because he reads no books and devotes no time to any sort of metaphysical thinking, his talks with his friends at the club are either about money, income tax, ways of cheating the Internal Revenue Service, sex, or about some silly joke or story which they found in yesterday's paper.

Yet, the Harry we meet in *Rabbit is Rich* is basically a happy man, despite his intermittent crises of confidence. For him life is seen as "just beginning, on a clear ground at last, now that he has a margin of resources" (89). Even his notion of freedom has changed now that he "wants less." "Freedom, that he always thought was outward motion, [turned] out to be this inner dwindling' (89). Yet, so happy is Rabbit with his inner dwindling, which is little besides his mental movements of readaptation to the new boundaries of the establishment's guidelines, that his son, Nelson, cannot tolerate it. It makes his father, paradoxically, look greater than he believes him to be and knows him to be.

Thus, although it is true that wealth brings to Rabbit a freedom that he had never enjoyed before, it is also true that in many respects he is as enslaved as ever, perhaps even more so. He is enslaved by the power of money and status, by his constant fear to lose what he has earned, or rather won, he is enslaved by his past weaknesses and mistakes, and by his intellectual limitations.

Money has made him, among other things, a member of the Flying Eagle Club and of the Rotary Club. He has also become a defender of the oil companies, a supporter of South Africa's apartheid system, although he does not phrase it that way, and a man conscious that he should always be with the rich, for he now knows that "when the little man climbs on the bandwagon the smart money gets off" (340).

And money made his religious convictions become more openly expressed, as if to remind us that money, law, morals, and religion do go hand in hand, and that now he is one of the hands. As the empathizing narrator tells us, "God, having shrunk in Harry's middle years to the size of a raisin lost under the car seat, is suddenly great again, everywhere like a radiant wind" (365).

But, besides religious, Rabbit has become a snob capable of denying support to old friends, because they are not club members and because they are not exactly rich. He shows off whenever he can and enjoys the "conspicuous vicarious pleasure" of "having a wife who can be at the club so much" (35). His house can no longer be in Penn Villas — it has to be in Penn Park, where "all those nice divorce lawyers and dermatologists [live]" (329). He even wants a street with his name, but refuses to accept the suggestion of "Angstrom Alley." He prefers "Angstrom Street," for, as we are told, he had enough of alleys in poor Mount Judge. Poverty is a past he wants to erase from his memory.

With money comes also the fear of losing it. Rabbit is especially afraid of Nelson who, having temporarily given up college, insists on working with him on the lot. His fear of Nelson as the competitor who wants to replace him and take his money seems to confirm Eccles's wife's Freudian analysis in *Rabbit, Run* and refers us back to Harry's jealousy of Nelson's relationship with his lover, Jill, in *Rabbit Redux*. But his fear seems also to be connected to the Hemingwayan notion that a man's fear of death is directly proportional to the amount of his wealth. This would

also explain why he feels better now that Skeeter is dead. Skeeter, as we have seen, believed that the American system was
essentially wicked and should be destroyed. As a defender of
this faith, now within the economic fortress of the system, Rabbit's fears are more understandable and real than ever. Nelson,
Skeeter, anything that threatens his position as "the king of the
lot" (3) should be kept as distant as possible.

Money has become such an obsession with Rabbit that he
even holds it responsible for his lack of sexual attraction for
Janice. In fact, Harry's self-analysis fails to see his fascination
with money and profits within the context of his other social and
cultural generalizations. Harry has difficulty in allowing himself
to think in terms of group interests in action in America,
although he is immersed in them, and perceives their existence.
And when he does, it is in relation to his higher ideal, America,
with capital A, in comparison to which all else is deformed.
Sexually, these high-level abstractions seem to make "real people [not] exciting enough" (329), and he prefers the idea of
Woman to the particular reality of woman — masturbation, thus,
having become a normal and acceptable way to sexual
satisfaction.

Harry's past is frequently brought up in *Rabbit is Rich*. His
glorious days when he was a basketball star, more than twenty
years ago, are reduced to yellowing newspaper clippings, and
the energy of the runs of *Rabbit, Run* has been exhausted by his
returns to Mount Judge and to Penn Villas. Physically, the agile
Rabbit has become a fat and ugly walrus. Soon, however, Mrs.
Springer, the owner of the house he still lives in, will not boss
him around any longer now that he, at forty-seven, decided that
he needs his own house. When read in isolation, this seems to
suggest the same move towards freedom of the previous two
novels. When read as a sequel, however, we immediately perceive that the move tends to send Rabbit more deeply into the
matrix of the establishment. By the end of the novel, Rabbit is a
man of the system who no longer needs to be guided or moth-
ered. He is stupidly reliable and has "conquered" the right to
enjoy its economic privileges.

Similarly, the trip to the Caribbean with their friends is not liberating at all, although Rabbit does feel more reconciled with the reality of sex. With a rare glimpse of understanding, Harry tells Janice that their sexual adventures should not be regarded as something to be condemned. For him, it was a little adventure of a group of conservative people — all members of their class — who decided to give expression to their sexual fantasies, something to be done on a tropical island, away from the pressures of society, away from home. As he tells Janice, "they're just like us. That was a holiday. In real life they're very square" (426). The sentence explains why Rabbit always returned after all his runs and sexual adventures in the previous novels. He was at that time already essentially "very square."

This roughly summarizes the novel's plot line and points towards the way the historic elements and events are selected and used by Updike. The primary use of historic material in the novel is to serve this story, a story which, however, is not meant to be only Rabbit's, but the story of a middle American man in the late seventies, a man carried along by events but whose home "is [still] like America used to be" (122)

The topical events contribute not only toward the creation of the appropriate mood for the environment in which Rabbit moves, they also help us understand the ideological spectrum Updike tries to portray, showing where in this spectrum Rabbit is meant to be seen. Although Rabbit has remained fundamentally the same, the range of the spectrum surrounding him has been significantly narrowed down, having almost returned to the uniformity of the fifties. But, because the presence of topical events in this novel is much greater than those referred to in *Rabbit, Run* and also in *Rabbit Redux*, one may have the false impression that the spectrum is much larger. In fact, the world of the seventies seems to have been significantly simplified when compared to the sixties, with the basic assumptions of the fifties gaining a new shine, having been repolished by the events of the Nixon and Carter Administrations. Thus, my reading forces a rewriting of Kathleen Lathrop's thesis that the theme of *Rabbit is Rich* is "the spiritual diminishment of modern man and his victimization by the very affluence his technology has created."[2] Lathrop's reading is quite accurate, but it overlooks the fact that diminishment implies a reduction in size, strength, or virtue, which cannot convincingly be said to be the case when Rabbit's assumptions are taken into account. The wrong turn was taken in 1959, twenty years earlier, and in *Rabbit is Rich* Rabbit is neither smaller nor larger, neither better nor worse, neither wiser nor more idiotic. His frame of mind, his thought structure, his underlying motivations, the things that make him tick are astonishingly similar in the now older and richer Rabbit, in an America faced with different realities. It is the "spiritual diminishment" which he accepted in the fifties which now is killing Rabbit, and it is because of that surrender that the Rabbit of the late seventies "can only think along certain lines" (108). That he has not grown wiser is more accurately his tragedy, for he remains victim of the same beliefs and illusions which have guided his life in earlier decades. The words of Lear's fool unavoidably come to one's mind when one thinks of Rabbit in *Rabbit is Rich*: "thou shouldst not have been old till thou hadst been wise."[3] Rabbit is a victim of this same misfortune. He has remained essentially static throughout the seventies and, therefore, is quite ill-equipped to face the events and the reality of the decade that is ending and the new decade that is beginning when we meet him.

It would be too lengthy a study to explore all topical events Updike discusses in *Rabbit is Rich*. The novel is a mosaic of American life, bringing to the foreground the popular culture of the decade, the scientific events, the international political arena, and the psychological and "economic life" of the average American. Thomas Edwards claims that *Rabbit is Rich* is "clearly a story of the economic life"[4] as opposed to the more social emphasis of *Rabbit Redux* and the spiritual emphasis of *Rabbit, Run*. Although somewhat oversimplified (as we have seen, the other novels also bring forth, in greater disguise, it is true, the economic base of Rabbit's conflicts), the statement does help us see that Rabbit's conflicts here have a more directly-related economic origin. No wonder then that we find the economic events dominating the novel.

Rabbit is Rich, like its two predecessors, is very precisely situated in time. The novel starts exactly on June 30, 1979, "late in the afternoon of this long last Saturday of June and the first of calendar summer" (4). The economic event that is affecting the life of Americans is the new 1979 oil crisis. Every aspect of American life seems to have been touched and transformed by it, from truck drivers, of whose strike the reader is constantly reminded, to car dealers, to the millions of car drivers throughout the country.

The most remarkable, and metaphorically extremely effective, sentence in the novel is the first. The opening statement, "running out of gas" (1), phrased the way it is, is ambiguous and refers both to Rabbit and to America. Both seem to be running dry — America because of the oil crisis, Rabbit because of his loss of sexual energy. In both cases, however, Updike is willing to suggest the presence of a false alarm, since neither the oil crisis nor Rabbit's sexual "dryness" seem to have to do with a true exhaustion of sources. Still early in the novel, Rabbit discovers that his sexual "well" is still productive, that "he hasn't come with such a thump in months. So, who says he is running out of gas?" (50). This energy will increase significantly throughout the book, reaching its highest point during his and Janice's swinging experience in the Caribbean. Similarly, also very early in the novel, the oil crisis is presented as a possible false alarm. Although Rabbit claims that "mother Earth is drying up" (5), Charles Stavros accuses him of refusing to see the obvious, namely that the oil crisis was a fabrication of the American government and the oil companies:

> "Listen, Harry. You know damn well Carter and the oil companies have rigged this whole mess. What does big oil want? Bigger profits. What does Carter want? Less oil imports, less depreciation of the dollar. He's too chicken to ration, so he's hoping higher prices will do it for him" (6).

In both cases, then, the dryness is meant to be seen as temporary, a result of external circumstances, something that can be undone. This analogy, at the very beginning of the novel makes the link between middle America and Rabbit unavoidable, invit-

ing us to see the common trends of the decade in the protagonist's attitudes and thoughts.

As we can see from the quotation above, Stavros and Rabbit
continue to voice different interpretations about America. It
could not be different with the oil crisis. Rabbit wants to believe
that the big corporations are too small to manage mother nature,
the same way he himself feels so many times incapable of controlling his own natural drives. Despite his club friends' conviction that "absolutely the government rigged the whole gas
shortage last June" (159), he claims the crisis is genuine. Stavros,
on the other hand, sees only greed, monetary lust in this crisis —
the same greed, the same lust he sees now everywhere in America. As he puts it, "the little man is acting like the oil companies
now. I'll get mine, and screw you" (5).

The newspapers and magazines of the period reflect this conflict of interpretations abundantly,[5] adding to the representativeness of Updike's text in that it quite faithfully represents the
public mood of the time. And that is where Charlie and Rabbit
go to find examples to argue their case. Charlie supports his
claim that the little people are behaving like the big corporations
with an example from the huge gas lines which can right now
be seen all over the country. Because gasoline is expensive and
hard to get now that the stations remain closed during weekends, all sorts of crimes and unheard-of violent incidents are
occurring. Charlie tells Rabbit about the wife of a station owner
who had her hip broken by a car at the gas station line, and how
people, instead of helping the woman and her desperate husband, used the chance to give "themselves free gas" (5). Rabbit,
too, had heard of the incident, but he finds it "hard to believe"
(5). Yet, he also has some weird stories to tell about gas line
behaviors, and he cannot help commenting on the fanaticism of
the public and their stratagems to get some extra cents of gas in
their cars, or how the "auto-supply stores are selling out of their
siphons" (12), because of the increasing number of people stealing gas.[6]

Thus, Rabbit's examples corroborate Stavros's observation
about the behavior of the little man. His belief in the established

institutions, however, is so adamantly unyielding that he cannot make Stavros's connections. Neither can he conceive of Charlie's suggestion of a fabricated crisis. Hopeless, Charlie tells him: "Shit, Champ, you never blame anybody. Skylab could fall on your head right now and you'd go down saying the government had done its best" (6). When one remembers how strongly Rabbit felt about the criticisms against the establishment in the sixties, it is not surprising to find him in the seventies a prey to the official versions of the oil crisis. According to the polls, sixty per cent of Americans thought of the crisis as a hoax at the service of the oil companies. Again, as in the sixties, Rabbit remains among the last pillars of institutional support and faith.

The oil crisis, besides serving to stimulate national jokes, like the one about the stupendous mileage Christopher Columbus "got on three galleons" (9), also helped to reconsider the use of big cars by most Americans. Like Rabbit, America is driving smaller cars, but not fully convinced that the big car is at heart truly replaceable. People trade-in their bigger cars in exchange for smaller Celicas, Coronas, Tercels, and Corollas, but very soon, during the span of the novel, selling large cars starts becoming good, sound business once more, generating within Rabbit a tension between his love of profit and his love of the country. This tension will not be solved in the novel but can be found there from beginning to the very end. Like so many Americans, Rabbit drives his Toyota but thinks nostalgically of the time, twenty years ago, when he left his wife and drove all the way down to West Virginia and back in one night. "Crazy. You couldn't do that now without going to the savings bank first" (9). Rabbit is ambiguously at pains trying to convince himself that the time for cars which remind you of "a toilet being flushed" (8) is over. Neither can he give up his money nor can he erase his memory.

Rabbit's nostalgia and the fact that many Americans despite the prices "still won't drive a little car" (9), preferring the "old boats, the Continentals, the Toronados" (207) indicates that America's love affair with the big cars of the fifties is not yet dead. His son Nelson's insistence on buying and selling older

and bigger cars has to do with his somewhat intuitive understanding of this widespread belief that "the old American cars"
(327) were the best, forcing one to remember "how great they
were" (327). Nelson's success at selling big cars during a time of
rationing confirms that Rabbit refuses to rationalize the American ambiguity that he himself expresses with regards to cars and
the oil crisis. With the historical perspective allowed us by our
seven years of distance from the 1979 crisis, one is tempted to
predict that by 1989, if Warren's diagnostic is right, he will have
forgotten the establishment's explanation that the oil crisis was
due to the drying out of oil wells, or that it was caused by the
Iranian revolution, or OPEC's price policies, and he will probably be facing the same conflict he now faces, i.e., he will enjoy
the profits he can make selling Japanese cars and he will enjoy
the comfort of the big American cars.

Although the roots of Rabbit's and Nelson's conflicts are many
and complex, having especially to do with the experiences both
have had together for the last twenty-three years, the conflicts
in *Rabbit is Rich* are also largely related to the oil crisis. Rabbit
considers Nelson reckless and spoiled, incapable of adapting to
the new reality of the country. Rabbit, unlike Nelson, is keenly
mindful, or at least he pretends to be so as long as it means
selling more Toyotas or saving a few dollars, of the national
energy-saving effort — the fifty-five mile per hour speed limit,
no gas on weekends, the odd or even car plate number, the gas
purchase limit, the low thermostat, carpooling, unnecessary
lights turned off — and he finds it unbearable to have a son who
does not take these things seriously, and worse, drives his car at
high speed in low gear.

Rabbit's awareness of the energy crisis does not leave him at
any moment. Although rich he is in constant need to save, and
he feels guilty when attracted to the superfluous, be it a three-
dollar can of cashew nuts or one too many bulbs lit in somebody's bathroom. "Going down with all her lights blazing the
great ship of America" (281), that is how he sees the wasteful
consumption of energy. At Nelson's wedding he feels irritated
by the procession of cars burning unnecessary gas, and later, at

his home, he questions Soupy, the minister, about the mileage of his Opel, reminding the Minister that the car is a contribution to the national waste of energy, prompting him to ask Rabbit if he is trying to sell him one of his Toyotas.

Similarly, when Janice and Mrs. Springer decide to replace Charlie Stavros for Nelson at the lot, Rabbit argues that there is no future there for Nelson, that he should go into the building of solar panels—"that's where the future is, not selling cars. Cars have had it. The party's over. It's going to be all public transportation twenty years from now. Ten years from now even" (243). Rabbit's argument is more interesting for its expression of a national concern with a search for alternative sources of energy than as a prediction worthy of our attention. In fact, not only is his argument disregarded by Janice and Mrs. Springer, but in all likelihood he himself does not fully believe what he is saying. What we have here is Rabbit parroting the in-vogue ideas about the alleged seriousness of the energy crisis, as he found them expressed in *Consumer Reports*, in the papers, or on television. As he does so often in *Rabbit Redux*, here, too, Rabbit's words are not his, and it takes little effort on the reader's part to perceive that the energy-crisis talk is being used to mask Rabbit's fears of having in Nelson not another source of income but an extra salary to pay. The effect is comic, not very different from hearing Rabbit tell Janice, after a week with Skeeter in *Rabbit Redux*, that the law "serves a ruling elite. More power to the people" (193). In either case, the words are not Rabbit's and his parroting is deliberate and cannot be taken as a serious argument.

Neither can we take seriously Rabbit's use of the energy crisis to convince Janice that they should move to "the other side of Brewer, closer to the lot [because] that drive through the middle of town is driving [him] crazy [and] wastes gas, too" (329). Although some gas could be saved with this move, we cannot help seeing that Rabbit is anxious to use the opportunity offered by Nelson's marriage to start a new life, away from the omnipresent "claws" of Mrs. Springer and away from Nelson's accusations and demands. The energy crisis is a red herring used here to camouflage Rabbit's true intentions. Nevertheless, it is an excellent illustrator of the mood generated by the specific economic reality of 1979. The energy crisis did not only make Rabbit rich, it also became the very motor of Rabbit's life. From beginning to end of the novel Rabbit will use the crisis to brood about his own gain and loss of energy, and, like America, he seems to embody the paradox of the period. When he thinks he is running out of gas, his life gains a new impetus, sexuality blooms again, money, as if through magic, is poured into his bank accounts, and freedom and the promise of a new beginning are there to be his, finally. Thus, in one word, it would be difficult to conceive of the present structure of *Rabbit is Rich* without the metaphorical use of the historic fact — the latter generates the former, confirming Updike's comment to Paul Gray, in *Time* magazine, that the idea for the third Rabbit novel only occurred to him after the energy crunch of 1979.[7]

The energy crisis, however, is not the only historic event to be employed as a catalyst of thoughts, words, emotions, and actions. The same applies to almost all the other topical events mentioned in the novel — the Edward Kennedy accident, the hostage crisis, the Pope's visit, the invasion of Afghanistan, the Carter-era inflation, the high price of gold, the American boycott of the Olympic games, the Panama Canal affair, the falling of the Skylab, the Shah's illness, the Three-Mile Island nuclear accident. The use of all these events as generative elements in the novel's structure and texture leads us to speculate that the story grew more out of history than the history out of the story, despite the previous existence of a plot line which required coherence, necessity, and plausibility.

The Edward Kennedy accident, for example, although it happened ten years earlier, has become news again because of Kennedy's decision to run against President Jimmy Carter for the Democratic Party's nomination. Unavoidably, his opponents would not miss the opportunity to bring the accident to the front pages of magazines and newspapers. *Rabbit is Rich* reflects this renewed national interest in the affair. As in the sixties, opinions continue to be divided. Charlie Stavros wants to trivialize the incident and wonders "how much more [they can] say about a guy on his way to neck who drives off a bridge instead" (95). Nelson's hippie friend, Melanie, also wants to dismiss the incident, adding that the conditions of the roads and bridges at the scene of the accident make one wonder how similar accidents do not happen more often. Realizing, however, that the whole incident has been transformed into a question of faith rather than of knowledge, lending itself too easily to partisan exploitation, Melanie prefers to praise Janice's "lovely soup" (96) instead.

Old Mrs. Springer, however, revives her dead husband's pro-Republican posture, namely that the senator is guilty either of murder or of irresponsible behavior, having fled the scene of an accident. Charlie, although his view on the issue seems to favor Kennedy, accepts Mrs. Springer's doubts and uses them to remind his little audience of Franklin D. Roosevelt's and Jack Kennedy's sexual affairs, with the implication that if Democrats could do such things, the suspicions which now fall upon Senator Kennedy have good reasons to exist. Again, as in *Rabbit Redux*, Stavros's loyalty is above the parties' politics. And Mr. Springer lives on through his wife, although without the same impetus and conviction.

For Harry the Kennedy incident serves an even more important role. Having lived for ten years with the nightmare of Jill's death, and being constantly accused by his son of having let her die, of being a coward, Rabbit instead of politicizing the incident personalizes it. Thus, Kennedy's tragedy becomes his tragedy, both men sharing the same sense of helplessness. As Rabbit puts it: "I never understood what was so bad about Chappaquiddick. He tried to get her out" (96). The narrator, with perfect identification, adds: "Water, flames, the tongues of God, a man is helpless" (96). This historic incident, then, is much more than setting — it is a device employed by Updike to allow his character to reevaluate his responsibility in past events at the same time as Americans are being forced to reevaluate the responsibility of one of their presidential hopefuls. Along with Rabbit, the reader, too, is asked to think back about the incidents and consider the

responsibilities. Somehow, by linking and likening the two incidents Rabbit's personal concern acquires a national dimension,
and his question, namely, what would I have done under similar
circumstances?, becomes the nation's question. Rabbit's answer
to this question comes across, therefore, as more than a jerk's
gratuitous search for self-justification—it is actually a search for
fairness in the judgment of a man made powerless by the force
of uncontrollable circumstances. Nelson's accusations and the
media's accusations and insinuations, become, a fortiori, the
expression of senseless and irresponsible criticism. History,
then, in this case, seems to be the Joycean nightmare Rabbit and
America are trying to awake from. Updike's view seems to be
that Kennedy's history redeems Harry and vice versa.

Nelson, however, will force us to reevaluate this posture of
the redeemed Rabbit. Without denying the truth of Rabbit's
interpretation of the Kennedy incident and of his own participation in Jill's death, Nelson forces us to see that the Rabbit of
the late seventies is more concerned with his solid-citizen image
than ever before, and that an even greater pro-establishment
deadness now guides his life. Nelson does have a good point
when he tries to explain to Pru that "Dad doesn't like to look
bad anymore, that was one thing about him in the old days you
could admire, that he didn't care that much how he looked from
the outside, what the neighbors thought when he took Skeeter
in, for instance, he had this crazy dim faith in himself left over
from basketball days, or growing up as everybody's pet or whatever so he could say Fuck You to people now and then. That
spark is gone" (293).

Thus, although the historical event in its specificity helps to
unload a burden that Harry had been carrying for years, it also
reveals the light uncommitted movements of the man whose
shoulders are clear. Nelson, one may argue, lacks authority to
pass judgment on his father, he himself being uncommitted and
destructive. One cannot help, however, giving him some credit,
for indeed Rabbit's concerns appear to be extremely self-serving,
making his nationalistic rhetoric vacuous, but then again is this
not Charles Wilson's rhetoric and Rabbit's belief in the fifties?

Nelson's discourse definitely invites us to connect Rabbit's past and present.

But, Updike's final decision to have Rabbit start his new life at an elegant dead-end street is certainly no coincidence and its associations with a road that leads nowhere, with a journey come to an end, with deadness are unavoidable. What Nelson does not perceive is that the Rabbit of the sixties to whom he refers was essentially a "solid citizen" gone astray for a few months and not a man who did not care about the community around him. What Nelson's mind has retained of the 1969 experience, thus, can hardly be said to be representative of the "domestic Rabbit" Harry has always been. Nelson's attempt to portray Rabbit as a social rebel is an absolute misrepresentation, probably stemming from his traumatic and affectionate memories of the days Jill and Skeeter stayed with them, days which may have masked the true conservative and guilt-ridden traits of Rabbit's character. Rabbit's "spark" of life in the seventies is, then, directed toward keeping the wealth he has managed to accumulate and to enjoy it as much as possible, without being "trapped, [like Carter and Khomeini], by a pack of kids who need a shaving" (331).

Updike's stress on Rabbit's false sense of commitment, in fact, gains new strength when the Iranian hostage crisis is brought into the novel and stays there. Rabbit has already profited from the Iranian revolution because of the reduction of Iranian oil exports to the United States; now, with the American hostages being held in Iran, the Arabs have started investing in gold, pushing its price to unprecedented heights.[8] But, because everybody is buying gold, Rabbit is told by his friend Webb Murkett, who seems to understand quite well the intricacies and fine threads of the market's web, that it is time to leave the gold and buy silver. And so Rabbit does, making very good profit. What is interesting here, however, is not the nature of Rabbit's investment, but Updike's open and unequivocal suggestion that investors like Rabbit have an interest in keeping the hostage crisis going. Rabbit has not yet taken the just-purchased silver coins to his bank's safe deposit before he realizes that should "the Iran thing get settled...the whole bubble [might] burst" (343). Thus, Rabbit perceives that for him the hostage crisis is useful and he is glad that he has made the right investment at the right time, and secretly he wishes that it will go on for a little while longer, for if the political instability ceases, the depreciation of silver may follow and mean a significant loss. On the other hand, as Webb says, "silver could double, if they don't return the hostages" (343), and that would mean a significant profit. Just as with the oil crisis, which Stavros, Murkett, and Inglefinger had identified as a fabrication of economic interests, the hostage crisis, too, it is suggested, has its beneficiaries, who might wish to see the solution to the crisis postponed a little longer. And Harry Angstrom, whose old sense of guilt has been fading away lately, is one of them.

The same way the Iranian hostage crisis fills the pages of the book, so does the Pope's visit to America. As it happens with the hostage crisis, the visit of the Pope is more than background. Besides precisely situating the novel's action in time, the event is appropriated by Updike's characters and used to generate action.

Because the Pope's visit is television news long before he actually arrives, Rabbit has a feeling that perhaps finally now, in the "wonderful country [of his] middle age" (214), things are beginning to happen — perhaps the very meaning of life, which had been hiding for so long. "Not only is the Pope coming but the Dalai Lama they bounced out of Tibet twenty years ago is going around the U.S.A. talking to divinity schools and appearing on TV talk shows, Harry has always been curious about what it would feel like to be the Dalai Lama" (214). The meaning of life seems to be in these events, in the kinds of things we can see in front of us, on TV, in daily life. "It's not something you dig for but sits on top of the table like an unopened dewy beer can" (214), waiting to be opened and consumed, an object of our desires.

At night, at home, in front of the television, we find Janice and Rabbit discussing the money wasted on the construction of a platform from which the Pope would deliver one of his masses to the thousands who will come to listen to him on October the third. The news is that "in Philadelphia, publishing magnate Walter Annenberg has donated fifty thousand dollars to the Catholic Archdiocese to help defray costs of the controversial platform…Annenberg, the announcer gravely concludes, is a Jew" (230). Janice cannot understand why the announcer had to refer to the fact that the donor was a Jew. Rabbit's reply is charged with anti-semitism: "to make us alleged Christians feel lousy we've all been such cheapskates about the Pope's platform" (230). The answer also tells us that for Rabbit the Pope's visit is of great importance. Rabbit is reminded that there is something like Christianity which unites a large portion of humanity, to which the Jews do not belong, and to which he himself only allegedly, not truly, belongs. Pope John Paul the Second becomes the symbol of this unity.

Because of this identification with the Pope, Rabbit accompanies his trip on television throughout the country with great interest. When the Pope arrived in Boston, Rabbit asks Charlie if he thinks "it's going to rain on the Pope" (251), to which Stavros replies: "Never. He'll just wave his arms, and the sky'll be full of bluebirds. Bluebirds and horseshit" (251). The narrator's comment says it all : "though no Catholic, Harry feels this is a bit rude" (251). The Pope is in Rabbit's eyes a sacred religious leader and should be taken as being above the vulgarities of the world. For Stavros the Pope is a common man, without magical powers, a rhetorician who can only convince a crowd of fools.

This same sort of conflict around the Pope's visit occurs during a party at Webb Murkett's home between his wife Cindy, an alleged Catholic, and Peggy Fosnacht, with whom Rabbit had a love affair ten years earlier. At the party, they discuss the Pope. Peggy, outraged by the Pope's statements against sex outside or before marriage, against women in the priesthood, and against abortion, starts an argument with Cindy. The two women in fact do not disagree so much about the Pope's obvious sexist rhetoric or about his outdated sexual rules, but Cindy is offended by Peggy's way of so aggressively criticizing the supreme authority of the church according to whose doctrine she was educated, especially because Peggy, not being a Catholic, does not owe any allegiance to the Pope.

Cindy's being hurt by Peggy's words reproduces Rabbit's hurt feelings, a little earlier, because of Stavros's rude joke. Both have sacralized the Pope's image and what he represents. Thus, whereas Rabbit is impressed by the Pope's good English, "about his seventh language" (256), Peggy takes the content of his English and tries to put it into the perspective of an American reality of the seventies, when women are fighting for the Equal Rights Amendment, when divorce is common practice, when pre-marital and non-marital sex is rampant, when birth control is the norm, when abortion is legal, when "fuck movies" (277), as Ronnie Harrison refers to the pornography shops, have become an integral part of the citiscape. Indeed, considering this reality of the America of the seventies, one would think that the Pope is talking to a small minority of Americans and that Peggy's arguments should cause no controversy at all. That it does can only be understood because of Cindy's sentimental attachment to a world of strong stands and magistral authority—a world which she cannot totally abandon, reason why she still goes to mass, even though she is married to a divorced man, practices birth control, and joins the other members of the group in their exchange of sexual partners. As with Rabbit, Cindy has an underlying faith in the established institutions, a faith which little adventures among friends on a Caribbean island cannot destroy. Her criticism of the "American liberals in the church" (268) is also an expression of her longing for a stronger authority and more rigid rules of social behavior, here symbolyzed by the Pope.

The devolution of the Panama Canal, which coincided with the Pope's arrival, seems to fall under the same category of concerns, in that it, too, stresses the weakening of America's power and authority in the world. Even Stavros, who in the sixties criticized America's abuse of power throughout the globe, now regards America's powerlessness as something regrettable. "I get sick of the news," he tells Harry, "this country is sad, everybody can push us around" (251).

What Stavros means by "everybody" is made clear not so much by the novel's text as by its context, forced into the novel by the time specifications. Stavros's observation precedes the hostage crisis, so that the reference is to events which preceded it. What could they be? The 1979 oil crisis might be one, although Stavros earlier did not seem to believe that OPEC was the artificer of the crisis. That leaves us with another major event, namely, the Ayatolla's revolution and its anti-Americanism. America's deep involvement with the Shah, which would precipitate and extend the hostage crisis, caused not only major embarrassment but also meant the total loss of America's political and economic influence in Iran. This is most certainly what Stavros had in mind in October 1979.

What one is forced to speculate about is why a revolution like the Nicaraguan, which also meant the loss of American influence, is only present through one single phrase, which could easily pass unnoticed by most readers, for it is never repeated or commented upon. We repeatedly hear references to the Shah's wanderings, the doubts about his health problems, his hardships in exile, but only once, at one single moment, do we hear something about Somoza's ordeal. The Sandinista's victory and their anti-Yanqui posture are never mentioned. Although this event, because of its contemporaneity, could very well have been referred to in the text to help stress the crumbling of America's power in the world, it is not. The Central American event seems to have been overshadowed by the more powerful Iranian controversy. The overthrow of the Nicaraguan Somoza dictatorship by the revolutionary Sandinistas is only present through its conspicuous absence, an absence which one cannot fail to notice if one accepts the novel's invitation to contextualize and historicize its actions. Charlie's remark that "everybody" can push America around seems to suggest that even countries without expression, countries you do not even have to bother to mention, can do it.

The Soviet invasion of Afghanistan is an action-generating topical event which also stresses the powerlessness of America in the seventies. At the Springer Motors lot, Rabbit and Nelson discuss the event. Rabbit's reaction seems to be a mixture of anger and satisfaction now that "those Russkins...sure gave themselves a Christmas present" (353). Nelson, however, points out to Rabbit that, wrong as it is, the Russians, unlike the Americans in Vietnam, "do it, when they're going to do it. We **try** to do it and then everything gets all bogged down in politics. We can't do **anything** anymore" (354). Rabbit agrees with Nelson that indeed that is the way America seems to be right now, but for him the explanation is not in the political institution, but in the unwillingness of people like Nelson to fight. As we can see, he has changed very little since the days of *Rabbit Redux* when he blamed America's lack of success in Vietnam on the hippies, the blacks, and the national unrests in America's cities. Now, Rabbit goes as far as accusing his son of getting married "to stay out of the next war" (354). Nelson's disbelief in America's strength, however, is such that he promptly replies that there will be no other war, that, as with the hostages, "Carter will make a lot of noise, but will wind up letting [the Russians] have [Afghanistan]" (354). Whereas the Pope becomes a symbol of the stability, sacredness, and power of an institution, Carter, even to Rabbit, becomes a symbol of powerlessness. Afghanistan and Iran are, then, intricately knitted into the novel's texture. They are outside events that Carter with all his wealth and might cannot control. Like Rabbit, America is rich. Like Rabbit, America is having trouble keeping and protecting the wealth and power it gained.

Another topical event brought up in the novel is the Three-Mile Island nuclear accident. Its action-generating power, however, is almost non-existent. We know that Peggy Fosnacht is going to participate in an anti-nuclear demonstration and Ronnie Harrison, ridiculing Ollie Fosnacht, tells him that he heard that "the Vatican and Three-Mile Island are hand-in-glove" (276). The event, probably because it had already a smell of yesterday's paper and was worn-out by more recent news, generates no more action. This explanation, however, might be too simplistic, especially when we recall that in *Rabbit, Run* the notorious Argus experiment coincided precisely with the story's timing and was also conspicuously ignored. The answer for this lack of exploration of such a hot topic, especially since the movie with Jane Fonda and Jack Lemmon, *The China Syndrome*, released one week before the accident, had such a tremendous impact on the nation, can probably only be provided by Updike himself. As with the Nicaraguan revolution, Three-Mile Island, although mentioned, is almost exclusively present through the novel's demand to be historicized. Apparently Updike did not see how he could have more deeply integrated the event into the plot and still maintain his fidelity to the truly nationally representative. Even if Updike considered the topic a mere fashion, it still remains surprising that he did not give the anti-nuclear demonstrations a larger space in his novels' reproductions of radio and television news broadcasts. It seems as if a deliberate decision to avoid the issue was taken by Updike already in the late fifties and reaffirmed in the seventies. Whatever the reason for this almost total blackout on the nuclear problems in the nuclear age, imperceptible traces seem to have been left within the covers of the three Rabbit novels. After all, history seems to serve the purpose Updike wants it so serve, no more and no less.

Many other references to specific events are present in *Rabbit is Rich,* and few of these have little significance to the story as a whole. One could be tempted to argue that they do little more than help form the social scenario in which the characters move, a scenario which already without these particular pieces of news would have been more than satisfactorily depicted. But, a closer look will show that we are not only dealing with Updike's eagerness to transcribe with precision the social and psychological milieu of the times, saving no words to get his verbal picture painted, but that, taken together, these pieces of news do add to the picture of the novels' themes or concerns.

Let's consider, for example, the following re-creation of a typical *Rabbit-is-Rich* news broadcast:

> The four-thirty news: earthquake in Hawaii, kidnapping of two American businessmen in El Salvador, Soviet tanks patrolling the streets of Kabul in the wake of last Sunday's mysterious change of

leadership in Afghanistan. In Mexico, a natural-gas
pact with the United States signals possible long-
term relief for the energy crisis. In California, ten
days of brush fire have destroyed more acres than
any such fire since 1970 (229).

Except for the earthquake in Haway and for the California
brush fires, all the other pieces of news are easily perceived as
part of the major concerns of the novel, namely the state of the
American economy and its international politics. At a broader
level, however, even the two disasters are not unrelated. As we
pointed out before, the pervading theme of the book, i.e., America's powerlessness, its being like Rabbit, "a fortune's hostage"
(437), "fortune" meaning both wealth and fate, is present also
in these kinds of disasters. The oil crisis itself, despite the insinuations about corporate economic maneuverings, is ultimately,
as Rabbit and Melanie point out, although with different interpretations, also a disaster involving mother nature running dry,
a "disaster" like discovering that old age is approaching, that
the sexual well is running dry, that a horrible cancer is taking
over, and that one is helpless.

Thus, there seems to be a theme-determined criterion even in
Updike's choice of news which apparently have no structural or
textural significance. This pattern generally requires little effort
to be seen, and shows that little if any of the selected history is
gratuitous. In fact, the news broadcasts are always presented to
us by the empathizing narrator through Rabbit's mind, with the
obvious implication that we hear or read what matters to Rabbit,
the history which he has appropriated. Since Rabbit's major worries are all related to his "fortune" — all the news he selects and
which the narrator tells us about are related to his being a hostage of this "fortune" of his. But, because Rabbit's ordeal so
much parallels America's, his experience ceases to be individual
to become representative of the nation as a whole.

Rabbit's "fortune" is so obviously jeopardized by the younger
generation — "the kid's growing up [seeming] a threat and a
tragedy to him" (128), showing up just about everywhere,
"making the music, giving the news" (432) — and by the fluctua-
tions of the dollar, the oil crisis, the international political con-

flicts, that one tends to overlook the other more national social forces which hold him hostage.

First, it should be said that the Rabbit of *Rabbit is Rich* has a history of his own which starts playing a very important role in the development of the novel, especially because his past experience is being constantly evaluated in the light of present events and circumstances. This applies to his trip twenty years ago to West Virginia, now, because of the high prices of gasoline, considered by Rabbit himself a little economic madness, as it applies to issues such as the rights of blacks and women, the hippie culture, nationalism, communism, or war. These issues are all reconsidered in *Rabbit is Rich*. And mostly they all seem to tell us that, although the country has changed, the changes are only cosmetic, superficial, and that both Rabbit and the country remain fundamentally the same.

In the sixties Rabbit sheltered a black man in his home and kept him there until his home caught fire and burned down; he also, after their short affair, helped him keep out of trouble by driving him out of the white community; in the seventies all direct contact with blacks has disappeared. He sees them when he drives through downtown, and he meets a few of them at his lot now and then. They are buyers, whom Rabbit mentally ridicules for having dressed up for this special occasion, and for being unable to realize that the "gas-hogs" he is unloading upon them are not worth the money. Nelson and Pru also go to parties where blacks can be found, but they have little or no contact with them. Skeeter and his revolutionary message have become ghost-like, an image of threat which from time to time haunts Rabbit, but which, most of the time, disappears among his most immediate concerns. All in all, blacks in *Rabbit is Rich* remain apart from the white society, almost unnoticed, and when noticed they become the target of ridicule and prejudice, a prejudice which is by no means only Rabbit's. Nelson, Mrs. Springer, and other characters in the novel also show the same kind of attitude.

Nelson minds the couple of "blacks mooching around so superior, that decided cool way they have of saying hello, daring you to outstare them, not taking responsibility for anything though, [making] him itch with fury" (301). Nelson is also angered by the fact that one of Pru's dancing partner's "has been one of the sassy Brewer blacks" (303), and he argues with his father that Pru, at the hospital, should have a room of her own, for in the ward where she is "one of [the women] was even black" (322).

Mrs. Springer also seems to have no appreciation for blacks or jews. When she first heard of Nelson friend's name, Melanie, she was definitely against receiving her. Throughout the discussion, it becomes evident that part of her fear is that Melanie might be black: "Melanie, what kind of name is that? It sounds colored" (40).

Harry's prejudices, however, are expressed throughout the novel, indicating Updike's concern to give the black-white relationship started in *Rabbit Redux* some continuity by trying to tell us what happened to it. And what Updike is telling us in *Rabbit is Rich* is that middle America regards the black man as inferior, incompetent, dangerous, and sloppy—a disgrace to America. Downtown is to be feared and avoided. "Blocks and blocks of blacks" (241) invaded whole sections of the city, and Rabbit, although he has some personal satisfaction in seeing the blacks admiring his car, prefers to "like everybody with [his] car windows locked" (75). Although he feels safer with Skeeter dead, he still fears that "Skeeter lives" (408), for he knows that Skeeter hated everything he stood and stands for, especially now that he buys Krugerrands and pretends to himself and to Janice that by doing so he is creating jobs for poor South African blacks. His fear of Skeeter, then, seems to be the fear of his personal destruction. Now Rabbit is no longer a supporter of the system; he is one of its pillars—the declared target of Skeeter's rage.

His fear of Skeeter may also be understood as a result of Rabbit's incapacity and unwillingness to identify the causes of America's problems within the establishment forces. The same way he, in the sixties, blamed the American failure in Vietnam on the blacks, hippies, and foreigners, he now blames the blacks, drugged and zonked "jigaboos wearing headphones pumping music into their ears" (325) for the "lousy cars" (325) put into the market by Ford. Thus, Rabbit is able to generalize the negative things he sees in individuals of a race but he cannot generalize his respect for the wisdom of individuals of the same race. His prejudice becomes even more patent when he refuses to see what everybody around him seems to be telling him, namely that big cars are not being bought only by black dumdums, but by all those people all over the country who can still afford them. Thus, what Harry regards as black ignorance can only be read as plain prejudice, probably resulting from his associations of blacks with poverty, an association which, Updike seems to be telling us, is slowly being subverted, to the astonishment of middle and white America. Ironically, the well-being of blacks brings economic benefits to Rabbit, which seems to suggest that Rabbit is not so much afraid of being mugged by blacks as he is afraid of the change of the power relation between the races. As is common with Rabbit in similar conflicts, he identifies with the dominator, stressing again his inveterate conservatism and resistance to change, despite spasmodic flirtations with it.

Nowhere is this inherent conservatism more evident than in the establishment's absorbtion of the hippie movement. Unlike the sixties, when the hippie culture was anti-establishment, allied with the civil rights movement and openly against the Vietnam war and the excessive consumerism of the decade, in the seventies, the hippies as a force of protest have disappeared and have mingled with the establishment. As Lance Morrow pointed out, "with a speed at least startling and at worst scandalous, the decade absorbed the 60s extravagantly experimental sexual mores into the main currents of American society."[9] As with the sexual mores, most of the hippie ideas and behaviors were brought into the system.

This phenomenon of absorption can be observed in the attitudes, things, and behaviors which have changed significantly since the sixties. While buying his silver, Harry notices, for instance, that "funny how [the hairstyles have] swung completely around: the squares let their hair grow now and the fags and punks are the ones with the butches. Harry wonders what

they're doing in the Marines, probably down to their shoulders"
(344). Harry's perception of this fashion change shows that the
hippies did leave their mark on the establishment, the punks
having become the non-conformist posture. The hippies, or
rather, "these ex-hippies[,] are everywhere, trying to hang on"
(212), opening little "leather-working plants" (212), transforming their hand-made leather shoes, bags, and sandals into mass-
produced industrial commodities.

Similarly, the hippie ideas about health were absorbed by the
system in a number of ways. Vegetarianism, homeopathic medicine, meditation schools, and health stores can be found all over
America. As Charlie Stavros observes, "the fitness industry has
become big bucks. Remember all those little health-food stores
hippies used to run? You know who runs'em now? General
Mills" (8). Thus, although the new hippie type, as represented
by Melanie, does seem to have some alternative proposals to the
crises of America, her views hardly go beyond the hippie proposals of the sixties, and these views have, most of them, been
transformed into fashion commodities with mainly marginal
penetrability. They will be tolerated, commercially explored, in
some cases enjoyed even, but they will come and go, leaving
their mark on the surface of the system, not in its core, more **on**
people's head than in it. Rabbit, like middle America, absorbs
the forces of change but discards them just as easily once they
have outlasted their exchange value or threaten the very existence of the system. Jill and Skeeter had a use value, fertile,
revolutionary, which middle America and Rabbit have annihi-
lated, neutralized, and almost completely forgotten. Their survival in the seventies depends almost exclusively on the
system's capacity to commercialize the non-essentials of their
proposals.

Rabbit's greatest dilemma in *Rabbit is Rich* is perhaps his having to sell foreign cars in the country he loves so much. His
nationalism, at least in words, is as strong as it was in *Rabbit
Redux*, and it is a true irony that the Japanese are behind his
wealth and not Ford or Chrysler or General Motors. As he tells
his customers, "Here we're are supposed to be the Automobile

Heaven and the foreigners come up will all the ideas. If you ask me Detroit's let us all down, two hundred million of us. I'd much rather handle native American cars but between the three of us they're junk. They're cardboard. They're pretend" (13).

This dilemma characterizes very well the "crisis of confidence" in himself as well as in America, to which Paul Gray dedicates a whole article. It bothers Harry that the Japanese influence is so pervading, so much in fact that he discovers himself using centimeters instead of inches as if it were the American way. And if things don't change, soon "he'll be talking Japanese" (20). But what seems to bother him most, despite his obvious profit with the present crisis, is that "people are going to loose faith in the system" (21). And for him America is still the only, the best, the one truly free country in the world. That he has to sell Japanese cars and buy a Sony TV for his new house is particularly troublesome. The last two pages of the novel express this concern of his with a wonderful image. Rabbit is at his new home, lying on his new bed, and falls asleep. "In his dream he and Charlie are in trouble at the agency, some crucial papers with some numbers are lost and where the new cars should be in the showroom there are just ragged craters, carefully painted with stripes and stars, in the concrete floor" (435). This was obviously the work of nationalists like himself, and who probably interpret his line of business as a betrayal of America. He wakes up feeling as if "somebody had slugged him in the face with a ball of wet clothes" (435). But he is middle America, and middle America is today hooked to the television set, watching the Steelers and the Rams. Soon he is all cheers, along with the Californian cheerleaders who at half time sing: "Energy is people, people are en-er-gy!,...flashing sheets like tinfoil that are supposed to be solar panels" (436). Harry's nationalism awakens again, more energetically, as if his crisis of confidence is over for ever: "Who needs Khomeini and his oil? Who needs Afghanistan? Fuck the Russkis. Fuck the Japs for that matter. We'll go it alone, from sea to shining sea" (436). But there is no indication that this rhetoric will somehow translate itself into action. The contradiction is still there. On Monday Rabbit will be back at his lot selling Japanese cars, probably not without a little discomfort in his chest.

With these things in mind, it is impossible to accept Kathleen Lathrop's contention that "*Rabbit is Rich* is the most hopeful of the Rabbit series."[10] She attributes this alleged hopefulness to the fact that "it is a novel of generations."[11] However, even as a novel of generations, it is hard to find any indication of hope in *Rabbit is Rich*. Nelson comes through as a jerk, a father who like his father abandons his wife while she is pregnant and does not even care to return for the child's birth; he is portrayed as reactionary, pretentious, selfish, careless, weak, asocial, intellectually mediocre, and full of racial prejudice. If there is any hope, it certainly cannot be found in Nelson.

The birth of Nelson's daughter at the end of the novel is insufficiently explored for us to be able to say that she represents something beyond the unknown future. All we have, in fact, is Rabbit's perception that his granddaughter is "another nail in his coffin. His" (437). The granddaughter is his and the coffin is his; in other words, Rabbit's death and his continuity are assured in the same sentence. His daughter is just one nail in his coffin, the other, one tends to see as Nelson or even his daughter, who may very well not **be** his daughter. Yet, even as Rabbit is getting ready for his death, the seeds of middle America are being planted to assure its own continuity. Nelson has already started the process. We are told what it looks like and we are led to believe, even told, we could argue, that the prospect for the future with Nelson does not look very promising. What Nelson's daughter will be like only time can tell. At the end of *Rabbit is Rich* she is no doubt on the train of America, but she is a light in the caboose, illuminating nothing except herself.

Updike's greatest negativism seems to be expressed, however, in Rabbit's extravagant new home at his dead-end Harry Angstrom Way. Its mirrors and bathrooms with toilet paper printed with comic strips seem to indicate that Harry has definitely jumped on the bandwagon of waste and superfluousness. What Updike is suggesting is that the road to salvation is in E. F. Schumacher's "Culture of Poverty" and not in *Consumer Reports* or *Beautiful House*. Rabbit's own observation, earlier in the novel, that "the world keeps ending but new people too dumb to know it keep showing up as if the fun's just started" (81) applies very well to Rabbit himself. The path of waste he has finally appropriated is a dead-end street and, although it may mean the beginning of a life of fun, it is, for sure, also "another nail in his coffin. His."

Notes

[1] John Updike, *Rabbit is Rich* (New York: Fawcett Crest, 1981) 2. (All further references to this novel are cited parenthetically in the text).

[2] Kathleen Lathrop, "Updike on America: The Expanding Vision of John Updike in his Post Olinger Novels," diss., New York State University, 1984, 221.

[3] William Shakespeare, *The Tragedy of King Lear.* (New York and Scarborough, Ontario: Signet, 1963) 74.

[4] Thomas Edwards, "Updike's Rabbit Trilogy," *Atlantic*, 248 (October 1981): 100.

[5] In TS 691 of *Rabbit is Rich*, at Harvard's Houghton Library, we find an enormous amount of research material utilized by Updike. Along with photocopies of a whole book on the ideal used-car salesman, fliers from car dealers, copies from *Automotive News*, maps, calendars, etc., one finds also a copy of a long article entitled: "Was the Gas 'Crisis' nothing but a fraud?" The article was taken from the Boston Sunday Globe, September 23, 1979. Its author is Fred J. Cook, and the article carries the following lead: "The great oil crisis of the summer of 1979 may well go down in history as one of the greatest frauds ever perpetrated on a helpless people. The truth is that there was no shortage." This article which Updike made a point to deposit along with his manuscripts indicates that Rabbit's and Stavros's discussion comes directly out of the reality of the scene. It also confirms my view that Rabbit's lack of political suspicion comes from his sacralization of authority, which simplifies his reading of the social text. (In TS 691 of *Rabbit is Rich*. Cambridge: Houghton Library, Harvard).

[6] MS 691 offers us one of the sources of Rabbit's examples of people's behavior at the gas lines. One source which is worth mentioning, among many others, is the piece of news from the *Boston Sunday Globe* (July 8, 1979), whose lead reads as follows: "the nation's first gasoline riot, not surprisingly, occurred at the point where the American Dream met the energy crisis." This is the headline: "The Day They Ran out of Gas." The Article was written by Sidney Blumenthal, and it is illustrated by pictures subtitled: "a demonstrator watches as flames shoot from a burning car during last month's gasoline riots in Levittown, Pa." There are also pictures of truckers on strike, carrying placards, two of which read: "to hell with Shell" and "Rationalize or Nationalize." As we can see, the very first sentence of the novel, "running out of gas," probably

was taken from Blumenthal's article. Updike's need to preserve this material for posterity is certainly an attempt to inform his critics on his scene-oriented methodology, with little disguised hope that this understanding may lead to a different interpretation of his work. The extensive documentation which accompanies the seven manuscripts and typescripts of *Rabbit is Rich* corroborates my interpretation that Updike's work should be read with an emphasis on scene rather than on hero.

[7] Paul Gray, "A Crisis of Confidence: *Rabbit is Rich*," Rev. of *Rabbit is Rich* by John Updike. *Time*, 5 Oct. 1981: 90.

[8] Along with MS 690 of *Rabbit is Rich* is a table with the values of Gold for the days of January 7, 8, and 10, 1979. All these values were used as basis for his computations of his purchase of silver in the novel on those same days, pointing once more to Updike's remarkable realistic concerns.

[9] Lance Morrow, "Epitaph for a Decade," *Time* 7 Jan. 1980: 38.

[10] Kathleen Lathrop, "Updike on America: The Expanding Vision of John Updike in his Post-Olinger Novels," diss., New York State University, 1984, 222.

[11] Ibid. p. 222.

Conclusion

"I can understand both his anger and his passivity."

(*Picked-up Pieces*).

A question that should be entertained again at the end of this discussion is "what would one miss if one failed to see the scenic elements of the Rabbit trilogy?" My flat answer, after all that has been said, is that one would miss the point. However, I believe the question deserves a longer answer as well. One could claim, for example, that it is possible to read *Rabbit, Run* as the story of a man who (one day?) decides to leave his wife. He ends up living with a prostitute for about three months, but when his wife is about to have his baby, he is ridden with guilt and decides to return home. After a week home, he can stand his life no longer and flees again. His wife then gets drunk and accidentally drowns their baby. At the funeral, feeling blamed for the baby's death, he reacts against the accusations and runs again.

This is the storyline of *Rabbit, Run* stripped of almost all scenic elements. One may find it interesting, enjoyable, and one may sigh and say "how sad and how beautiful," and one may even insist, supported by the broad shoulders of the millenary wisdom of Aristotle, that this is the very soul of the work. My argument, however, is that, essential as it is, this is not the soul but a dead skeleton, a structure which is lifeless unless life is given to it by the flesh and spirit of the scene. In the Rabbit trilogy this spirit and flesh starts being added to the skeleton of the novels as soon as the novels' characters, actions, and motions are placed precisely in time and space, adding to it, so to speak, the breath of life. Thus, it makes all the difference in the world to know that the story takes place in an American town, in 1959, and not in a small town in the Brazilian pampas. The scene specifications are so important that one immediately perceives, by such rather extreme scenic dislocations, that were it not placed where it is, Rabbit's story would have been quite different, and we would not be surprised if instead of riding his car we would have found him riding a horse. The freeways would have become trails, his map the stars, the gas attendant, that divine messenger of the Hamiltons, well, he could become a grassy field by a river. With some imagination this could go on for ever. Joyce showed us very clearly what a modern Odysseus would be like, were he in Dublin in 1904. Like Leopold Bloom, he would not kill his wife's lover and he would not defend the status quo; he might even be a masturbator. And his physical fitness would be far less important than the quickness of his intellect, for the Cyclop's rocks have become, in Dublin, a can of biscuits.

No matter how much one tends to read the new in its association to the old, and one can hardly help doing so, the fact remains that one is never in any danger of confusing Homer's Odysseus with Joyce's Bloom. Similarly, one would have to recognize the uniqueness of Updike's Rabbit as opposed to a similar character placed in another reality. Updike's Rabbit is not atemporal or ethereal. He gains his life from the air he breaths, the cars he drives, the roads he travels, the parking lots he sees, the games he plays, the gadget he sells, the used cars he sells, the television programs he watches, the radio news broadcasts he hears, the people he talks to, in one word, the scene.

Few critics have denied the importance of the scene in Updike's novels, but few have been willing to attribute to it the force Updike meant it to have. It is this unwillingness to grant the scene its due strength and dynamism that led Yves Le Pellec, in an interesting article called "Rabbit Underground," to wrongly predict that, after *Rabbit Redux* "Updike [would] probably not wake [Harry] up again, for a third Rabbit might be a Rabbit Redundant."[1] Le Pellec's mistake reveals a perception of Harry as too static a hero to deserve a sequel. Although my findings confirm this perception, they also reveal that Rabbit's interest lies not so much in himself as in the relationships he is somehow condemned to establish with his environment. And because the environment Updike reconstructs is an arena of conflicts, where major national events, moods, and ideologies, come to life, even a common man, in the relationships he perforce establishes with this text, has to gain interest. This does not, as one could hurriedly suppose, deny Rabbit his individuality or make him mechanistically a product of his environment. Instead, it places greater emphasis on his social entrapment, on those social features which make him a creature of his time and place, a representative man rather than an eccentric freak. As Michael Novak remarks in an article cleverly entitled "Son of the Group," Updike portrays the middle-class, things, behaviors, and actions that surround us, "our supermarkets and their parking lots, our ranch houses and the sloshing scotch and ice of neighborhood parties, our churches and the pressure of death beneath our skins." And he concludes: "it is startling to recognize how seldom **our** lives have been made the stuff of literature."[2] Updike's scene, in the Rabbit trilogy and in most of his novels, is not only overwhelming, it is also representative of the scene upon which middle America lives its life.

Thus, the answer to what we would miss without accepting Updike's precise placement of the novel in time and space is that one would fail to perceive the very thing that gives life to the novels and to the characters. One would also fail to perceive the tension-generating technique which made Updike's protagonist in the Rabbit trilogy palatable and the novels such a success. The essentially static agent is placed upon an essentially dynamic social text, generating moods which go from the tragic, through the awkward, clumsy, ridiculous, pitiful, to the outright comic. That this variety of moods is possible shows that the dramatistic principle, put out by Kenneth Burke, that "the nature of the acts and agents should be consistent with the nature of the scene"[3] is valid both in its observation and in its violation.

This brings us to the second question: what is the nature of the scene in the Rabbit trilogy? I have argued that the scene is not only the starting point for action but also that it generates actions, motions, discussions, thoughts, expressions, attitudes which go beyond the realm of the individual. Thus, the individual Harry Angstrom appropriates, so to speak, the concerns of his national community and in so doing acquires representativeness, becoming emblematic of the time and place he lives in. In *Rabbit, Run,* in the late fifties, the historic acts are expressed as scene through the overwhelming presence of cars, freeways, gas stations, parking lots, shopping malls, the universal presence of TV, the gadget economy, the references to wars, the presence of topical events such as the Chinese invasion of the Dalai Lama's Tibet and the Eisenhower/MacMillan summit. This information comes to us as a social map, a representation of scene, rather than as particular historical events. The same way we are able to trace Rabbit's route from Reading to West Virginia and back on the night of March 20, 1959, we are also able to reconstruct the socio-economic, cultural, religious, and with some imagination, the political panorama within which Rabbit moves. The various components of this scene are incorporated into Rabbit's discourse and filtered through his mind frame which is nostalgically placed in the victorious days of the late forties and early fifties. Although he does not categorically oppose them, he still makes them into a source of his gripes against the system in transformation, revealing his regret that things no longer are in their manifestations what they used to be in the good old days of his youth. In the sixties, after Rabbit has accepted to readapt to the establishment's ways, despite its recognized deadness and second-ratedness, some of his fears have materialized. Television has become more popular than ever, having reached the moon; women have indeed abandoned their exclusive housewife role and started joining the job market and having their own affairs; friends are divorced; and the standards of sexual morality have undergone significant relaxation, sex having become a cheap and abundant commodity. New significant forces, however, have emerged and invaded Rabbit's home, either directly or through television: the landing on the moon, Ted Kennedy's car accident, the technological advancements which take Rabbit's job, the Vietnam war, the black movement, the hippie movement, and, finally, the beginning of what Kevin Phillips would call a decade later "the balkanization of Amer-

ica."[4] These forces triggered not only the novel (Updike con-
fessed that he decided to write a sequel to *Rabbit, Run* only when
he felt overrun by the events of the sixties), they also served as
the locomotive which would put Rabbit and the train of middle
America in motion. Rabbit's inveterate conservatism which had
remained somewhat disguised in the fifties and therefore wasn't
perceived by most critics, came to light in *Rabbit Redux,* and so
did also his sense of impotence in face of the powerful events at
the end of the sixties. The scene was very different from the
previous decade; some of the trends, which had their roots in
the fifties acquired such impetus that the conservative Rabbit
felt like going to the street with Nixon's "silent majority." He
participated in no protests against the protests which occurred
daily all over the nation, but he did not hesitate to make his
opinions clear to everybody no matter where or who they were,
and he would make a point in expressing his love for his country,
which for him is symbolized in a willingness to die for the country and in the love for the flag. Thus, with a Joe-Kelly kind of
fanaticism,[5] he began to exhibit a decal of the American flag on
his car window.

The nature of the scene in the sixties is, then, different from
the fifties in that the country is facing unprecedented social division, with groups of varying ideological nuances challenging the
central authority. What should be perceived is that Rabbit's position against change and for established authority becomes more
evident in *Rabbit Redux* than it does in *Rabbit, Run* because the
issues are still too much alive, and the internal division is making the country incapable of fighting a war it is engaged in and
which is tearing it apart. In the fifties Rabbit had gripes against
the things that he feared harmful to the unity and first-ratedness
of the nation; in the sixties, he has serious, extremely serious,
concerns. The nation is indeed, so it seems, tearing apart. President Johnson himself showed the country that he knew it, and
in a symbolic gesture, to set the example, abandoned partisan
politics to dedicate himself entirely, during his last months in
office, to the reunification of the country. Rabbit's concern is also
Johnson's. As in the fifties, then, Rabbit is an establishment

figure, anxious to preserve the existing institutions in their ideal state, protecting them from abuses and second-ratedness. The Rabbit of *Rabbit Redux* is a continuation of the earlier one and not an inversion as almost every critic has tried to make him. When one remembers that Rabbit is more a believer than the minister himself, that his love for the sacredness of the family is what takes him back to Janice, that he also loves Ruth because she is a woman who still can cook, that he believes in family duty so much that he is willing to start a fight at the bar in order to protect his sister, when we remember all this, we have little difficulty in perceiving how the "domestic Rabbit" and the "solid citizen" are one and the same person. The scene is different, but the social position and the fundamental attitudes of the Rabbits continue to be same.

Rabbit is Rich offers an even more obviously history-driven protagonist. As in the previous novel, Rabbit is carried by the events. This time, however, he is not a victim but a beneficiary. The 1979 oil crisis and the little Japanese Toyotas which he sells have made him rich. But his wealth has also made him a "hostage of fortune." Like Carter, Rabbit, too, is being held hostage by kids barely old enough to understand the full meaning of their deeds. The Iranian hostage crisis and Rabbit's conflicts with his son Nelson, who wants to "invade" his fortress and "take" his money, run parallel. Also Jimmy Carter's "crisis of confidence" speech is appropriated by Rabbit who uses it to explain especially his lack of sexual interest, his "running out of gas." His money, his wealth, he thinks, has also something to do with it. Sexually, too, he seems to be a hostage of fortune.

My chapter on *Rabbit is Rich*, then, also attempts to show the consistency of Updike's technique of presenting a rather static protagonist against a dynamic scene. The large amount of topical events of this novel, the thickest of the three, has the double purpose of presenting us with the new relation between Rabbit and the old forces of the sixties, and to present him facing the most recent political, economic and technological realities.

What is remarkable to notice in *Rabbit is Rich* is that the progressive forces of the earlier decade have simply vanished. The blacks have taken over the downtowns of cities and Rabbit and Nelson still resent their universal presence; the hippies have been absorbed into the system and are making money like everybody else; and even the female liberation thrust seems to have subsided, despite the legalization of abortion, divorce, the widespread use of birth control devices, and the fights for the Equal Rights Amendment. Janice is back in the kitchen and so are her female friends who spend most of their days at the Club. Ruth, too, decided to accept a life as a housewife.

Politically, America in 1979 seems to have reverted to the unity of the early fifties. In fact, Rabbit and his friends hardly talk about politics unless it has to do with international affairs, especially America's relation to communist countries. National divisions are no longer representative, although the ghost of Skeeter still seems to hover in the area. The after-effects of the loss of the Vietnam War, added to the recent "losses" of Iran and Nicaragua to anti-American regimes, seemed to be the political dimension of the country's crisis of confidence. Almost everybody has become more conservative—blacks, hippies, teenagers, Nelson, Rabbit, and even Charlie Stavros. *Rabbit is Rich,* in its stress on the increasing American conservatism, anti-communism, and nationalism, makes a wonderful forecast of the advent of Reaganism and its "America-is-standing-tall-again" policies. Be that as it may, Rabbit, more integrated to the establishment than ever, respects the man in office, the institutionalized authority, the president, regardless of the political party he represents. And if the President recovers God, that little raisin, from under the car seat, so does he; if he jogs, so does he, if he is a hostage, so is he, if he tells him that he, Rabbit, has a crisis of confidence, it must be true. As we can see, the fundamental pro-establishment attitude has not changed since the fifties, and if Rabbit is happier now, although it certainly has to do with the money he is making, it no doubt has to be especially attributed to the fact that for the first time in twenty years the America of his youth is finally within reach. That Updike made him become a Rotary-club member is indicative enough of how good a spokesman for the forces of conventional wisdom he has become and of the high level of integration he has achieved. Rabbit's perception of the Rotary Club members as grown-up kids also shows that the spirit of his generation, the "class of '51," has become dominant. Thus, Rabbit is no longer only a defender of the faith, he has become the faith itself, and to defend the establishment has now, more than ever, become a purely self-serving gesture.

Thus, the nature of the scene in each of the novels of the trilogy is directly related to the historic events during the three decades. The ten years that separate each of the novels mean time enough to characterize three quite distinct and unique moments in American life, and just enough time to allow for a sense of continuity, letting us perceive how Rabbit's America of the last decade spills over into the next. In fact, Updike's strategy of starting out the trilogy with a protagonist who is trying to recover at the end of a decade a scene, (symbolically present in *Rabbit, Run* through his victorious basketball days), placed in the past, sets the whole trilogy upon the polarity of past and present, conservation and change. And in this game we find Harry, like middle America, struggling to face the challenges of the present with a team of veterans. Or, more metaphorically put, Rabbit is very much like a sponge filled with water, and which every now and then is squeezed by reality and forced to absorb the new surrounding liquids. Although frequently squeezed in the last twenty years, it has remained as absorbent as ever and has insisted on being a sponge and refused to "run dry."[6] But it is also of the nature of a sponge to remain "intolerant" and "indifferent" to all that which is not liquid, that is, not appropriate for absorption. The implications of this is that the revolutionary nature of movements such as black power, hippies, and feminism can only be absorbed in their "liquidity." The Skeeters, who preach the destruction of the system, will have to be marginalized and eventually put to death; the sons which threaten the father's authority and hold him hostage will have to be resisted; the women who question the sexism of the Holy Father had better be kept in check.

The question which one has to ask oneself now is where Updike, the author, stands in all this. His narrator is most of the time so close to Harry Angstrom that one easily forgets that the novels make use of third-person narration. The America that we see, then, is through the eyes of a narrator whose mind and emotions seem to be almost identical to Harry's, as if the narrator had fallen in love with his character and is willing to portray his follies and conflicts with the surrounding scene not only with empathy but also with sympathy. The narrator seems to be telling us that he shares Rabbit's worries, weaknesses, and joys, because they are also in many ways his own, and the America Harry reacts to is, for good or for bad, also his own. Looking at America through Harry's eyes makes it seem all the more his own, and, like Henry Bech in *Bech is Back*, he probably would not like criticism of his country coming from Americans who went to live in Canada to avoid being drafted. They lack the emotional ingredient necessary to love a fellow citizen, something which Harry has more than anybody else. The narrator's admiration for Harry has largely to do with his honesty and determination to stay in the scene and fight it out there, reason why, perhaps, he was never "allowed" to escape. His honesty and determinations are in themselves generally likeable, his decisions and wisdom, not always.

Updike's concerns, which I fully identify with the narrator's, are, however, with portraying a middle American in his relations to America and the world. And what his portraits reveal is that, although America changed from decade to decade, her assumptions have remained fundamentally unchanged. Each major force deserves attention and deserves to be treated with candor and yet with honesty because all of them compose the broader picture of America. Because totality is humanly impossible to achieve, the portrait includes, as we have seen, major representative details for each decade. It is only through this synecdochical and metaphorical representation that a sense of completeness can be achieved, a sense which I would argue is the narrator's and Updike's primary objective, an objective which can be confirmed both in his fiction and non-fiction. Books like *Problems,* for instance, which in one of its pieces describes America as "a great conspiracy to make you happy,"[7] and *The Coup,* which is a view of America from Africa, are just two other apt examples of this attempt to portray America not only in time but also from different perspectives.

This, however, does not eliminate the question of ideological preference. In the fifties, for example, we are being asked to share Rabbit's fight against second-ratedness and against all those forces which threaten the scene which eight years before had given him and his community so much joy; the predominant ideological preference is for Rabbit; in the sixties, Charlie Stavros comes through as the only viable political alternative left for America—an alternative liberal enough to accept the blacks and hippies in the country and also liberal enough to understand the absurdity of the Vietnam war and other American involvements throughout the planet, yet not too liberal to accept the discourse of destruction of the system. Little wonder, then, that in the seventies we find Stavros quite reconciled with Rabbit, as if they had become accomplices in a game determined to save America. Stavros still seems to be an acceptable alternative, but his physical weakness, his weak heart barely allow him to survive. His gradual decrepitude may well stand for one aspect of the "spiritual diminishment" which Kathleen Lathrop identified in *Rabbit is Rich.*[8] In the seventies, however, one perceives a greater detachment from Harry than in the the previous two novels, and the reader gets the feeling that Rabbit's nightmares, pettiness, and folly are being diagnosed by a narrator concerned with an America which has learned to spend too much and has too little control over the forces which generate or threaten its wealth. America is wealthier but also more trivial and wasteful. The narrator one hears has less the voice of Stavros this time and more the voice of a Jimmy Carter: "In a nation that was proud of hard work, strong families, close-knit communities and our faith in God, too many of us now tend to worship self-indulgence and consumption."[9] Like Jimmy Carter, the narrator seems to be worried that the sacred values of mainstream America are being threatened by the "growing doubt about the meaning of our own lives"[10] trivialized by a crisis of abundance. The nation in *Rabbit is Rich* and the nation itself seem to be diagnosed by voices which are ideologically very close to each other. The narrator, too, like most of America has become more conservative. The historic and the literary as always in Updike's work run hand in hand.

Regardless, however, of our attempt to ideologically define the painter who is peeking from behind the portrait, the fact remains that Updike manages if not to hide at least to disguise himself among the colors of the background. We definitely see better the portrait than the painter, better the creature than the creator. This Stephen-Dedalus theory is also Updike's. Despite his obvious preferences for certain characters, behaviors, and ideas, most of the time, he, too, "like the God of creation, remains within or behind or beyond or above his handiwork, invisible, refined out of existence."[11] And this capacity to create and suffuse himself throughout the work of creation, as a sort of universal residual energy, can be attributed to Updike's acceptance to somehow become one with the thing created, while at the same time allowing himself to remain exiled from his created universe, not necessarily "paring his nails," but certainly protecting himself from easy and naive factional absorption. Plato would have called this multiple identification madness; Ion would have called it inspiration; I believe it should be perceived as the meticulous and passionate recreation of the spirit of America, in all its diversity and complexity. Updike reminds one of Aristotle's advice to his students in *Parts of Animals*:

> It remains to treat of the nature of living creatures, omitting nothing, whether of higher or lower dignity. For even in the case of creatures, the contemplation of which is disagreeable to the senses, Nature, who fashioned them, nevertheless affords an extraordinary pleasure to anyone with a philosophic disposition, capable of understanding causes. Hence, the consideration of the lowlier

forms of life should not excite a childish
repugnance.[12]

This is very similar to Updike's expressed wish "to transcribe
middleness with all its grits, bumps, and anonymities, in its
fullness of satisfaction and mystery."[13] Updike's text is so well
planted in the reality of the last three decades that, as Kathleen
Lathrop puts it, it will "undoubtedly earn Updike a place in
literary history at least as the chronicler of a generation."[14] And
his is an America where not everything is smooth, not everything is pleasant to contemplate. Sometimes in fact it seems very
bumpy and disagreeable to the senses, but most critics and readers, because they have Aristotle's "philosophic disposition,"
have not been repelled by "childish repugnance." These are
readers that understand that Updike's text is a portrait and a
study of the representative intricate relations between living and
dead "creatures" of America. And, because the object of the
study is middleness, America may indeed not be a fact but an
average; it may, as Updike says in *Problems*, be only "an act of
faith, a matter of lines on a map and words on paper, an outline
it will take generations and centuries more to fill in," a work of
art to be continued. If that is so, Updike has started writing it.

Thus, the awareness of incompleteness, the recognition of a
plan, an artistic construct, the admission of an act of faith—all
these allow Updike to deneutralize the American reality even
before actual selection has occurred, even before it is put to the
service of a conceived plot. And when, finally the net has been
cast and the representative sample has been chosen, the mode
becomes synechdochic and metaphoric, reduction and perspective having been added.

This study could have been, more appropriately perhaps,
called "The Power of the Scene in Updike's Rabbit Trilogy." My
choice of the present title, however, allowed me to place greater
emphasis on those historical events to which the trilogy refers
and to show how they fit the scene which is necessarily historical
as well, although the specific events and constituents that created it are not expressedly there. Thus, in *Rabbit, Run* I had to
rely more on scene because of the absence of numerically signif-

icant topical events. In the last two novels the direct reference to actual events of national impact is all-pervasive, and scene and historic data are so closely linked that one can hardly think of separating them even for didactic purposes. As it is of the nature of human action to occur in time and space, so it is a necessity to view them together and as inseparable. The events work as effective time and space referents, and the scene can be viewed as the presence of acts and agents in time and space. The national division of the sixties is, then, a mood which results from the conflicts between agents. The events one hears on television anchor those conflicts in time and space and, in so doing, bring the scene to life. Obviously, then, the events are only part of the scene. And, because Updike's scene is brought into the novel through specified time and space referents I did, and believe one should, for all practical purposes, regard the scenic and the historic as synonymous, for in studying Updike's trilogy one should not be concerned only with how events act upon Rabbit but also with how the historically-situated moods, motives, and values interfere with his life.

The argument that not all events are historic does not have to be doubted, once verifiability of the occurrence can be established. What was my concern, however, was the need to accept as historic that which Updike declared as such through its precise contextualizations. Fritz Stern's *The Varieties of History* (1956), for example, illustrates how different authors in different times differ in their ways of writing history. As Stern puts it:

> In the last analysis what will shape a particular history is the historian's conception of the past, whether or not he has formulated it, whether or not he is fully conscious of it.[16]

This "particular history" is not only the result of a particular mode of emplotment, but also an expression of the historian's selection of details. But what details should be selected remains incognito. Both Stern and Carr offer some guidelines as to what should be selected, but what they ultimately tell us is that anything that allows the present to better understand the past could be raised to the status of a historical fact. The historian says

Stern, "must always accept the fact that the choices he makes…are not of consequence to him alone, but will affect the moral sense, perhaps the wisdom, of his generation."[17] Carr also sees history as having the same double function, i.e., "to promote our understanding of the past in the light of the present and of the present in the light of the past."[18] Faced with a multitude of facts, "the historian selects those which are significant for his purpose, so from the multiplicity of sequences of cause and effect he extracts those, and only those, which are historically significant; and the standard of historical significance is his ability to fit them into his pattern of rational explanation and interpretation."[19] In other words, one remains with a selection which serves the purpose of a story being told, which is, as I tried to prove, exactly what Updike's methodology seems to be, except for the more obvious fictional plot which the selections serve.

Hayden White's *Metahistory: The Historical Imagination in Nineteenth Century Europe* (1973) and *Tropics of Discourse* (1978) are similar attempts at showing that to historicize means to add perspective, reduction, representation, and emplotment of facts, in one word, it means to deneutralize the world of events. White's language at times shows impatience with "historians [who] continue to treat their 'facts' as though they were 'given' and refuse to recognize, unlike most scientists, that they are not so much found as they are constructed by the kinds of questions which the investigator asks of the phenomena before him."[20]

It should be stressed, however, that Updike's view of history as a deneutralization of facts can be seen not only in the inner life the events acquire in their absorption by the fictional (for example, Ted Kennedy's car accident comes to mean to Rabbit that a man is helpless under certain circumstances whereas to Mr. Springer it means that Democrats are unreliable people), but also in various of Updike's comments and interviews. An often-quoted interview with Charles Thomas Samuels in the *Paris Review* and published again, along with six other interviews, in *Picked-Up Pieces* (1966) shows that Updike cannot conceive of his work as ahistoric:

Samuels: "So far as I can see, American history is normally absent from your work."
Updike: "Not so; quite the contrary; In each of my novels, a precise year is given and a President reigns; *The Centaur* is distinctly a Truman book, and *Rabbit, Run* an Eisenhower one. *Couples* could have taken place only under Kennedy...My fiction about the daily doings of ordinary people has more history in it than history books, just as there is more breathing history in archaeology than in a list of declared wars and changes of government.[21]

What Updike sees as giving life to events is, then, not their mere listing, not their classifying or cataloging, but their contextualization and emplotment, the digging for meaning, for the inner life they acquire in the actuality of a real or mimetically constructed experience. And this inner life always discloses our need to find consistency between agents and scenes, a consistency which Kenneth Burke considered naturally necessary for the human drama to unfold. The same way "*Couples* could have taken place only under Kennedy," each of the novels of the Rabbit trilogy expresses the spirit, "the social currents" of the time and space they are placed in. It is impossible to read the trilogy and not see three different decades of American history being brought to life. And if the America Updike portrays is not always smooth and pleasant, but oftentimes bumpy, ugly, and gritty, as we have seen in the chapters on the individual books of the trilogy, it is because the reality of life and the truth of America, during the last three decades, have been portrayed with a realism which is neither the nationalistic patriot's, the black militant's, the civil rights advocate's, the Republican's, the liberal's, nor the hippie's, nor the woman's, but of all of these at the same time, brought together with an all-inclusive Whitman-esque embrace, by a social painter[22] who loves them so dearly that he can show us their folly, their dramas, their tragedies, their cruelties, and their weaknesses, and still manage to convince us that what he wants is not to condemn or condone but to understand. In his "Afterword" to *Buchanan Dying*, Updike says: "I have sought to be the servant of what is known....the historical record has not been knowingly distorted or skimped."[23] As we have seen, the same can be said about the Rabbit trilogy. And it is this appropriation of the social text, not only by the characters but by the author himself, which makes Updike's America not only a picture of truth, but also an expression of love. This is also why Updike can claim that it does not take him much effort to understand both Rabbit's "anger and passivity."

Notes

[1] Yves Le Pellec. "Rabbit Underground," *Les Americanistes: New French Criticism of Modern American Fiction*, Ira D. and Christiane Johnson, eds. (Port Washington, N.Y. and London: Kennikat Press, 1978) 94-109.

[2] Michael Novak, "Son of the Group," *Critical Essays on John Updike*. William R. Macnaughton, ed. (Boston: G. K. Hall and Co., 1982) 59.

[3] Kenneth Burke, *A Grammar of Motives* (Berkeley, Los Angeles, London: University of California Press, 1945) 3.

[4] Kevin Phillips, "The Balkanization of America," *A History of Our Time — Readings on Postwar America*. William H. Chafe and Harvard Sitkoff, eds. (New York, Oxford: Oxford University Press, 1983) 353-364.

[5] Richard Rogin, "Joe Kelly Has Reached His Boiling Point," Ibid. p. 277.

[6] John Updike, *Problems* (New York: Fawcett Crest, 1972) 58.

[7] Ibid. 56.

[8] Kathleen Lathrop, "Updike on America: The Expanding Vision of John Updike in his Post-Olinger Novels," diss., New York State University, 1984, 201.

[9] Jimmy Carter, "America's Crisis of Confidence," *A History of Our Time — Readings on Postwar America*, William H. Chafe and Harvard Sitkoff, eds. (New York, Oxford: Oxford University Press, 1983) 322.

[10] Ibid. 320.

[11] James Joyce, *The Portrait of an Artist as a Young Man* (Harmondsworth: Penguin, 1964) 215.

[12] Aristotle, *Parts of Animals*, In Marjorie Grene, *A Portrait of Aristotle* (Chicago: The Chicago University Press, 1964) 93.

[13] John Updike, *Assorted Prose* (New York: Alfred A. Knopf, 1974) 186.

[14] Kathleen Lathrop, Op. Cit. 224.

[15] John Updike, *Problems* (New York: Fawcett Crest, 1972) 58.

[16] Fritz Stern, *The Varieties of History* (New York: Meridian Books, Inc. 1956) 13.

[17] Ibid. 32.

[18] Edward Hallett Carr, *What is History* (New York: Vintage Books, 1961) 41.

[19] Ibid. 138.

[20] Hayden White, *Tropics of Discourse—Essays in Cultural Criticism* (Baltimore: Johns Hopkins University Press, 1978) 43.

[21] John Updike, *Picked-up Pieces* (New York: Fawcett Crest, 1966) 482.

[22] Ibid. 51.

[23] John Updike, *Buchanan Dying* (New York: Alfred Knopf, 1974) 192.

Bibliography

Allen, Frederick Lewis. *The Big Change 1900-1950: America Trans-*
forms Itself. New York: Harper & Row, 1952.

Bakhtin, M. M. *The Dialogic Imagination.* Austin: University of
Texas Press, 1981.

Bakhtin, M. M. and Medvedev, P. N. *The Formal Method in Liter-*
ary Scholarship—A Critical Introduction to Sociological Poetics.
Baltimore and London: The John Hopkins University Press,
1978.

Barricelli, Jean-Pierre and Gibaldi, Joseph, eds. *Interrelations of*
Literature. New York: The Modern Language Association of
America, 1982.

Berthoff, Warner. *A Literature Without Qualities. American Writing*
Since 1945. Berkeley, Los Angeles, London: University of
California Press, 1979.

Burchard, Rachael C. *John Updike: Yea Sayings.* Carbondale and
Edwardsville: Southern Illinois University Press, 1971.

Burgess, Anthony. "Language, Myth, and Mr. Updike." *Com-*
monweal, 83 (11 Feb. 1966), 557-59.

Burke, Kenneth. *A Grammar of Motives.* Berkeley, Los Angeles,
London: University of California Press, 1945.

Burhans, Clinton, Jr. "Things Falling Apart: Structure and
Theme in *Rabbit, Run.*" *Studies in the Novel*, 5 (1973), 336-51.

Carr, Edward Hallett. *What is History?*. New York: Vintage, 1961.

Chafe, William H. and Sitkoff, Harvard, eds. *A History of Our*
Time. Readings on Postwar America. New York and Oxford:
Oxford University Press, 1983.

Chomsky, Noam. *Towards a New Cold War.* New York: Pantheon
Books, 1982.

_____. *Turning the Tide: U.S. Intervention in Central America*
and the Struggle for Peace. Boston: South End Press, 1985.

Cox, Harvey. *The Secular City: Secularization and Urbanization in*
Theological Perspective. New York: The Macmillan Company,
1966.

Dallek, Robert. *The American Style of Foreign Policy.* New York and Scarborough, Ontario: A Mentor Book, 1983.

"Desperate Weakling." Rev. of *Rabbit, Run*, by John Updike. *Time*, 76 (7 Nov. 1960), 108.

Detweiler, Robert. *John Updike.* New York: Twayne Publishers, Inc., 1972.

Dickstein, Morris. *Gates of Eden: American Culture in the Sixties.* New York: Basic Books, Inc., 1977.

Donaldson, Scott. *The Suburban Myth.* New York, London: Columbia University Press, 1969.

Doody, Terrence A. "Updike's Idea of Reification." *Contemporary Literature*, 20 (1979), 204-220.

Eagleton, Terry. *Marxism and Litrerary Criticism.* Berkeley: University of California Press, 1976.

_____. *Literary Theory: An Introduction.* Minneapolis: University of Minnesota Press, 1983.

_____. *Against the Grain — Essays 1975-1985.* London: Verso, 1986.

Edwards, Thomas R. "Updike's Rabbit Trilogy" Rev. of *Rabbit is Rich*, by John Updike. *Atlantic*, 248 (Oct. 1981), 94-102.

Elazar, Daniel J. "Meaning of the Seventies." *Society*, 17 (Jan./Feb. 1980), 7-11.

Ellison, James. "Rabbit is Buying Krugerrands." Rev. of *Rabbit is Rich*, by John Updike. *Psychology Today*, 15 (Oct. 1981), 110-15.

"Enemies of Promise." Rev. of *Rabbit, Run*, by John Updike. *Times Literary Suplement*, 29 Sept. 1961, p.648.

Enright, D. J. "The Inadequate American: John Updike's Fiction." In his *Conspirators and Poets.* London: Chatto & Windus, 1966, pp. 134-40.

Fairlie, Henry. "A Decade of Reaction." *New Republic*, 180 (6 Jan. 1979), 15-19.

Falke, Wayne. "*Rabbit Redux: Time/Order/God.*" *Modern Fiction Studies*, 20 (Spring 1974), 59-75.

Fleishman, Stanley and Rosenwein, Sam. *The New Civil Rights Act: What it Means to You.* Los Angeles: Blackstone Book Company, 1964.

Friedman, Murray, Ed. *Overcoming Middle Class Rage.* Philadelphia: The Westminter Press, 1971.

Galbraith, John Kenneth. *The Affluent Society.* Boston: Houghton Mifflin Company, 1958.

Gartner, Alan, and Frank Riessman. *The Service Society and the Consumer Vanguard.* New York, Evanston, San Francisco, London: Harper & Row, Publishers, 1974.

Gearhardt, Elisabeth A. *John Updike: A Comprehensive Bibliography with Selected Anotations.* Norwood, Penn.: Norwood Editions, 1978.

Gilman, Richard. "A Distinguished Image of Precarious Life." Rev. of *Rabbit,Run,* by John Updike. *Commonweal,* 73 (28 Oct. 1960), 128-29.

Gingher, Robert S. "Has John Updike Anything to Say?" *Modern Fiction Studies,* 20 (Spring 1974), 97-105.

Gray, Paul. "A Crisis in Confidence:*Rabbit is Rich.*" Rev. of *Rabbit is Rich,* by John Updike. *Time,* 118 (5 Oct. 1981), 90.

Greiner, Donald J. *The Other John Updike.* Athens, Ohio: Ohio University Press, 1981.

_____. *John Updike's Novels.* Athens, Ohio: Ohio University Press, 1984.

Haley, Alex. *The Autobiography of Malcolm X.* New York: Ballantine Books, 1984.

Hamilton, Alice and Kenneth. *The Elements of John Updike.* Grand Rapids, Mich.: Williams B. Eerdmans Publishing Company, 1970.

_____. *John Updike: A Critical Essay.* Grand Rapids, Mich.: William B. Eerdmans Publishing Co., 1967.

_____. "John Updike's Prescription for Survival." Rev. of *Rabbit Redux,* by John Updike. *Christian Century,* 89 (5 July 1972), 740-44.

Harper, Howard M. *Desperate Faith: A Study of Bellow, Salinger, Mailer, Baldwin and Updike.* Chapel Hill: University of North Carolina Press, 1967.

Hassan, Ihab. *Radical Innocence: Studies in the Contemporary American Novel.* Princeton: Princeton University Press, 1961.

Hicks, Granville. "Generations of the Fifties: Malamud, Gold, and Updike." In *The Creative Present: Notes on Contemporary American Fiction*, Ed. Nona Balakian and Charles Simmons. Garden City, New York: Doubleday & Co., Inc. 1963, pp. 213-38.

Hoffman, Daniel, ed. *Harvard Guide to Contemporary American Writing*. Cambridge and London: Harvard University Press, 1979.

Howard, John R. "The Flowering of the Hippie Movement." *The Annals of the American Academy of Political and Social Science*, 382 (March 1969), 43-55.

Howe, Irving. "Mass Society and Post-Modern Fiction." *Partisan Review* (Summer 1959), 428-36.

Hunt, George. "Updike's Rabbit Returns." Rev. of *Rabbit is Rich*, by John Updike. *America*, 145 (21 Nov. 1981), 321-22.

Jameson, Frederic. *Marxism and Form*. Princeton: Princeton University Press, 1971.

Jameson, Frederic. *The Prison-House of Language — a Critical Account of Structuralism and Russian Formalism*. Princeton: Princeton University Press, 1972.

_____. *The Political Uncosncious: Narrative as a Socially Symbolic Act*. Ithaca: Cornell University Press, 1981.

Johnston, Robert K. "John Updike's Theological World." *Christian Century*, 94 (16 Nov. 1977), 1061-66.

Kammen, Michael. *People of Paradox: An Inquiry Concerning the Origins of American Civilization*. New York: Vintage Books, 1973.

Kamenka, Eugene, ed. *The Portable Karl Marx*. Harmondsworth: Penguin, 1983.

Kazin, Alfred. *Bright Book of Life: American Novelists and Storytellers from Hemingway to Mailer*. Boston and Toronto: Little, Brown and Company, 1971.

_____. "Our Middle Class Storytellers." *Atlantic*, 222 (August 1968), 51-55.

Keniston, Kenneth. *The Uncommitted: Alienated Youth in American Society*. New York: Harcourt, Brace & World, Inc., 1965.

Kennedy, Eileen. "Rabbit Redux." Review of *Rabbit Redux*, by John Updike. *Best Sellers*, 31 (15 Dec. 1971), 429.

Klinkowitz, Jerome. "John Updike's America." *North American Review*, (September 1980), pp. 68-71.

Kohak, Erzim V. "Being Young in a Postindustrial Society." In *The Seventies: Problems and Proposals*. Ed. Irving Howe and Michael Harrington. New York: Harper & Row, 1972, pp. 151-68.

Kramer, Hilton. "Trashing the Fifties." *New York Times Book Review*, (10 April 1977), p. 3.

Lathrop, Kathleen. *Updike on America: The Expanding Vision of John Updike in his Post-Olinger Novels*. Diss. New York: New York State University, 1984.

LeClair, Thomas. "Updike's Anti-Metafiction." *Fiction International*, 4/5 (1975), 130-32.

Lipset, Seymour. "A Changing American Character?" In *Culture and Social Character: The Work of David Riesman Reviewed*. Ed. Seymour Lipset and Leo Lowenthal. New York: The Free Press of Glencoe, Inc., 1961, pp. 136-71.

Locke, Richard. *"Rabbit Redux"* Rev. of *Rabbit Redux*, by John Updike. *New York Times Book Review*, (14 Nov. 1971), pp. 1 ff.

London, Herbert. "The Counterfeit Decade: A Look Back at the 1970's." *USA Today*, 109 (July 1980), 11-14.

Lukacs, Georg. *The Historical Novel*. Lincoln and London: University of Nebraska Press, 1983.

_____. *History and Class Consciousness. Studies in Marxist Dialectics*. Cambridge: MIT Press, 1983.

Mallon, Thomas. "Rabbit, Jog." *National Review*, 33 (13 Nov. 1981) 356-58.

Mander, John. "In Defense of the Fifties." *Commentary*, 48 (September 1969), 63-67.

Markle, Joyce B. *Fighters and Lovers: Theme in the Novels of John Updike*. New York: New York University Press, 1973.

Millgate, Michael. *American Social Fiction:James to Cozzens*. New York: Barnes & Noble, 1964.

Mitchell, W. J. T. *The Politics of Interpretation*. Chicago: The University of Chicago Press, 1983.

Mizener, Arthur. *The Sense of Life in the Modern Novel*. Boston: Houghton Mifflin Company, 1964.

Morrow, Lance. "Epitaph for a Decade." *Time* (7 Jan. 1980), pp. 38-39.

Muse, Bejamin. *The American Negro Revolution: From Non-violence to Black Power 1963-1967*. Bloomington, London: Indiana University Press, 1969.

Novak, Michael. "Talk with John Updike." *New York Times Book Review*, (7 April 1968), pp.34-35.

O'Connell, Shaun. "Rabbits Remembered." *Massachusetts Review*, 15 (Summer 1974), 511-20.

Paterson, Thomas G. *On Every Front — the Making of the Cold War*. New York and London: W. W. Norton & Company, 1979.

Petter, Henry. "John Updike's Metaphoric Novels." *English Studies*, 50 (April 1969), 197-206.

Podhoretz, Norman. *Doings and Undoings: The Fifties and After in American Writing*. New York: Farrar, Straus & Company, 1964.

Potter, David M. *People of Plenty: Economic Abundance and the American Character*. Chicago and London: University of Chicago Press, 1954.

Pritchard, William. "In Clover: *Rabbit is Rich* by John Updike." New Republic, 185 (30 Sept.. 1981), 30-32.

_____. "Merely Fiction." Rev. Of *Marry Me*, by John Updike. *Hudson Review*, 30 (Spring 1977), 147-160.

Pritchett, V. S. "Updike." Rev. of *Rabbit is Rich* by John Updike. *New Yorker*, 57 (9 Nov. 1981), 201-206.

Raymont, Henry. "John Updike Completes a Sequel to *Rabbit, Run*." *New York Times*, 27 July 1971, p. 22.

Regan, R. A. "Updike's Symbol of the Center." *Modern Fiction Studies*, 20 (Spring 1974), 77-96.

Reich, Charles A. *The Greening of America*. New York: Random House, 1970.

Ricks, Christopher. "Flopsy Bunny." Rev. of *Rabbit Redux*, by John Updike. *New York Review of Books*, 16 Dec. 1971, pp. 7-9.

Riesman, David, with Nathan Glazer and Reuel Denney. *The Lonely Crowd: A Study of the Changing American Character.* New Haven and London: Yale University Press, 1969.

Rotundo, Barbara. "*Rabbit, Run* and a Tale of Peter Rabbit." *Notes on Contemporary Literature,* 1 (May 1971), 2-3.

Said, Edward W. *The World, the Text, and the Critic.* Cambridge: Harvard University Press, 1983.

Sale, Roger. "Rabbit Returns." Rev. of *Rabbit is Rich,* by John Updike. *New York Times Book Review,* 27 Sept. 1981, pp. 1, 32-34.

Sammons, Jeffrey. *Literary Sociology and Practical Criticism.* Bloomington: Indiana University Press, 1981.

Samuels, Charles. "Updike on the Present." Rev. of *Rabbit Redux,* by John Updike. *New Republic,* 165 (20 Nov. 1971), 29-30.

_____. *John Updike.* Minneapolis: University of Minnesota Press, 1969.

Sann, Paul. *The Angry Decade: The Sixties.* New York: Crown Publishers, 1979.

Sartre, Jean Paul. *What is Literature.* London: 1978.

Schopen, Bernard A. "Faith, Morality, and the Novels of John Updike." *Twentieth Century Literature,* 24 (1978), 523-35.

Searles, George J. "'Rabbit, Gun': Linguistic Evidence of Harry Angstrom's Self-Delusion." *Notes on Contemporary American Literature,* 8, iv (1978), 10-11.

Seigel, Gary. "Rabbit Runs Down." In *The Modern American Novel and the Movies.* Eds. Gerald Peary and Roger Shatzkin. New York: Frederick Ungar Publishing Co., 1978, pp. 247-55.

Sokoloff, B.A., and David E. Arnason. *John Updike: A Comprehensive Bibliography.* Folcroft, Penn.: Folcroft Press, 1971.

Standley, Fred L. "*Rabbit, Run:* An Image of Life." *Midwest Quarterly,* 8 (Summer 1967), 371-86.

Stern, Fritz, ed. *The Varieties of History.* New York: Meridian Books, 1956.

Stubbs, John C. "The Search for Perfection in *Rabbit, Run.*" *Critique: Studies in Modern Fiction,* 10 (Spring/Summer 1968), 94-101.

Suderman, Elmer F. "The Right Way and the Good Way in *Rabbit,
    Run.*" *University Review* (University of Mo. in Kansas City),
    36 (Autumn 1969), 13-21.

Taylor, Larry E. *Pastoral and Anti-Pastoral Patterns in John Updike's
    Fiction* Carbondale and Edwardsville: Southern Illinois Uni-
    versity Press, 1971.

"Ten Years that Shook America." *Newsweek,* 19 Nov. 1979, pp.23,
    ff.

Thorburn, David, and Howard Eiland. *John Updike: A Collection
    of Critical Essays.* Englewood Cliffs, New Jersey: Prentice-
    Hall, Inc., 1979.

Turner, Kermit. "Rabbit Brought Nowhere: John Updike's *Rabbit
    Redux.*" *South Carolina Review,* 8 (Nov. 1975), 35-42.

Updike, John. *The Poor House Fair.* New York: Fawcett Crest, 1958.

_____. *The Same Door.* New York: Knopf, 1959.

_____. *Rabbit Run.* New York: Fawcett Crest, 1960.

_____. *Pigeon Feathers and Other Stories.* New York: Knopf,
    1962.

_____. *The Centaur.* New York: Knopf, 1963.

_____. *Telephone Poles and Other Poems.* New York: Knopf,
    1963.

_____. "Comment." *Times Literary Supplement.* 4 June 1964,
    p. 473.

_____. *Olinger Stories: A Selection.* New York: Vintage Books,
    1964.

_____. *Assorted Prose.* New York: Knopf, 1965.

_____. *Of the Farm.* New York: Fawcett Crest, 1965.

_____. *The Music School: Short Stories.* New York: Knopf,
    1966.

_____. *Couples.* New York: Fawcett Crest, 1968.

_____. *Midpoint and Other Poems* New York: Knopf, 1969.

_____. *Bech: a Book.* New York: Knopf, 1970.

_____. *Rabbit Redux.* New York: Fawcett Crest, 1971.

_____. *Problems.* New York: Fawcett Crest, 1972.

_____. *Buchanan Dying: a Play.* New York: Knopf, 1974.

_____. "Introduction" to *Innocent Bystander: The Scene from
    the 1970's by L. E. Sissman.* New York: Vanguard Press, 1975.

_____. *A Month of Sundays.* New York: Knopf, 1975.

_____. *Marry Me: A Romance*. New York: Knopf, 1976.

_____. *Picked-Up Pieces*. Lond: Andre Deutsch Ltd., 1976.

_____. "The Cultural Situation of the American Writer." *American Studies International*, 15, No. 3 (1977) 19-28.

_____. "The Plight of the American Writer." *Change*, December 1977, pp. 37-41.

_____. *Tossing and Turning: Poems*. New York: Knopf, 1977.

_____. *Museums and Women and Other Stories*. New York: Alfred A. Knopf, 1978.

_____. *The Coup*. New York: Knopf, 1978.

_____. "One Writer's Testimony." *National Review*, 30 (26 May 1978), 641.

_____. "Saint of the Mundane." *New York Review of Books*, 25 (18 May 1978), 3-6.

_____. "Saddled with the World." *Scandinavian Review*, 67, No. 1 (1979) 68-71.

_____. *Too Far to Go: The Maples Stories*. New York: Fawcett Crest, 1979.

_____. *Rabbit is Rich*. New York: Knopf, 1981.

_____. "Updike on Updike." *New York Times Book Review*, 27 Sept. 1981, pp. 1, 34-35.

_____. *Hugging the Shore: Essays and Criticism*. New York: Vintage Books, 1984.

_____. *Roger's Version*. Alfred Knopf: New York, 1986.

Uphaus, Suzanne Henning. *John Updike*. New York: Frederick Ungar Publishing Company, 1980.

Vargo, Edward P. *Rainstorms and Fire: Ritual in the Novels of John Updike*. Port Washington, New York: Kennikat Press, 1973.

Vaughan, Philip H. *John Updike's Images of America*. Reseda, California: Mojave Books, 1981.

Walcutt, Charles Child. "The Centripetal Action: John Updike's *The Centaur* and *Rabbit, Run* and Wright Morris's *One Day*." In his *Man's Changing Mask: Modes and Methods of Characterization in Fiction*. Minneapolis: University of Minnesota Press, 1966, pp. 326-35.

Waldmeir, Joseph. "It's the Going That's Important, Not the Getting There: Rabbit's Questing Non-Quest." *Modern Fiction Studies*, 20 (Spring 1974), 13-27.

————. "*Rabbit Redux* Reduced: Rededicated? Redeemed?" In *Essays in Honor of Russel B. Nye*. Ed. Joseph Waldmeir. East Lansing: Michigan State University Press, 1978, pp. 247-62.

Ward, John A. "John Updike's Fiction." *Critique,* 5 (Spring/Summer 1962), 27-41.

Warren, Donald I. *The Radical Center: Middle Americans and the Politics of Alienation*. Notre Dame, London: University of Notre Dame Press, 1976.

Weber, Brom. "*Rabbit Redux*." Rev. of *Rabbit Redux,* by John Updike. *Saturday Review,* 54 (27 Nov. 1971), 54-55.

White, Hayden. *Metahistory: The Historical Imagination in Nineteenth Century Europe*. Baltimore: Johns Hopkins University Press, 1973.

————. *Tropics of Discourse: Essays in Cultural Criticism*. Baltimore: Johns Hopkins University Press, 1978.

Whyte, William. *The Organization Man*. New York: Simon and Schuster, 1956.

Wisse, Ruth R. *The Schlemiel as Modern Hero*. Chicago: Chicago University Press, 1971.

Wood, Ralph. "John Updike's Rabbit Saga." *Christian Century,* 99 (20 Jan. 1982), 50-54.

Yates. Morris W. "The Doubt and Faith of John Updike." *College English,* 26 (March 1965), 469-74.

Zinn, Howard. *A People's History of the United States*. New York: Harper and Row Publishers, 1980.

Index

Aldrin, Edwin, 81
Allen, Robert, 94, 100, 102, 110, 111
Angstrom, Earl: dominated by his wife, 56; Democratic posture, 82; anti-Republican posture, 84, 85
Annenberg, Walter, 129
Apolo 11, 6, 81-83, 86
Aristotle, 143, 153, 154, 158
Armstrong, Neil, 81, 83
Axes, 6, 7
Ayatolla Khomeini (see **Khomeini**)

Bakhtin M. M., xvii
Bech, Henry, xii, xix, 26, 151
Becky, 28
Bellow, Saul, 5
Bendiner, Robert, 93
Berryman, Charles, 110
Blumenthal, Sidney, 141, 142
Braudy, Leo, 33, 38
Breitman, George, 100, 111
Buchanan, 28, 102
Burchard, Rachael, xi, 11, 16, 17, 31, 37, 51
Burhans, Clinton, 50, 74
Burke, Kenneth, 1, 8, 9, 10, 11, 145, 157, 158

Carmichael, Stokeley, 94, 99, 101-103, 111
Carr, Edward H., 13, 14, 36
Carter, Jimmy: Rabbit identifies with Carter, xviii, 7, 132, 148; kids plaguing the Carter Administration, 7, 124, 127, 148; Carter and the oil crisis, 119; Carter and the hostage crisis, 124, 127, 148; Carter and the Russian invasion of Afghanistan, 124, 132; Carter and the narrator of *Rabbit is Rich*, 152, 153
Chappaquiddick (see **Kennedy, Edward**)

Charlie (see **Stavros**)
Chicago 8 Trials, 104
Chomsky, Noam, 71, 73, 74, 89, 110
Cindy Murkett, 35, 130
Cleaver, Eldrige, 103, 104, 111
Coach (see **Tothero**)

Dalai Lama: escape from Chinese forces, 6, 40, 41, 46, 47, 128, 146; Rabbit "is" the Dalai Lama, 6, 41, 42, 45, 46; the Dalai Lama's visit to the United States, 128
Dale, 10
Dallek, Robert, 93, 110
Detweiler, Robert, xix, 31-34
Dickstein, Morris, xv, 109
DuBois, W. E. B., 99
Dulles, John Foster, 49, 88

Eagleton, Terry, 41, 72
Eccles: and other Reverends, xi; the truth, xvii; the heaven-sent messenger 12; Rabbit's relation to, 33, 70; and Rabbit's "sanctity," 43-45; and marriage, 62; his wife's Freudianism, 115
Edwards, Thomas, 118, 141
Eiland, Howard, 36
Eisenhower, Dwight: Summit with MacMillan in Camp David, xiii, 6, 40, 46-48, 51, 146; and *Rabbit, Run*, 11, 26, 49, 157; and Janice, 56; Updike rewrites Eisenhower's words, 76; and McCarthyism, 88; and Indochina, 110

FDR (see **Roosevelt, Franklin**)
Fonda, Jane, 133
Fosnacht, Peggy: reference to Skeeter, 79; Rabbit's avoidance of Peggy, 108; divorce, 109; discussing the Pope, 129, 130; against nuclear energy, 132

Galbraith, Kenneth, 65, 74
Gold, Michael, 93
Greiner, Donald, xix, 13, 26, 31, 34-38
Grene, Marjorie, 158
Guevara, Che, 78

Hamiltons, Kenneth and Alice, xi, xix, 11-19, 26, 30, 36, 54, 144
Harrison, Ronnie, 55, 130, 132
Hearst, Patricia, 104
Heller, Joseph, 5
Hellman, Lilian, 87
Houghton Library, xiii, xv, xvi

Inglefinger, 128
Ion, 153

Jameson, Frederick, 2, 3, 10
Janice: Rabbit's return to Janice, 12; and Ruth, 21, 64; Rabbit reconciled with Janice, 44, 75, 79, 80, 108, 148; Rabbit's refusal to succumb to Janice's way of life, 55; and Eisenhower, 56; sloppy, 56; Janice's unwillingness to join Rabbit, 61; a "little mut," 62; Janice misses Rabbit's joke, 63; Janice's and Rabbit's car, 67, 68; Janice's addiction to TV, 69,70; why Rabbit left Janice, 69; Janice's "stubborn smallness," 70; how Janice sees Rabbit, 76, 77, 88, 107; Janice's decision to leave Rabbit, 78; Janice's affair with Stavros, 78, 109; pushy, 80; Janice and the moon landing, 83; Janice and the ideological spectrum, 99; Rabbit's fear of Janice, 108; Janice at the club, 113; Janice's sex appeal, 116; Janice's swinging experience, 119; Janice's decision to replace Stavros, 123; Janice's "lovely soup," 125; Janice and the Pope, 128, 129; Janice and Krugerrands, 136; Janice is back in the kitchen, 149
Jill: with Harry at the Burger Bliss, 7; and the ideological spectrum, xvii,
23, 99, 107; describing Rabbit, 28; Jill and the hippie counterculture, 29, 104, 107, 109; Jill as reality instructor, 75, 78, 101, 105; the society she hates, 78, 101, 105, 107, 138; Jill and Skeeter, 79, 138; Jill's death, 80, 125-127; the ambiguity of Jill's discourse, 106; Jill and Nelson, 115
Johnson, Arthur, 74
Johnson, Lyndon: criticized by Mr. Springer, 84, 86; division in the American house, 87, 93, 147; Rabbit identifies with Johnson, 88, 91, 92; the war motif, 92, 93, 110
Joyce, James, xi, 24, 144, 158

Keniston, Kenneth, 66, 73
Kennedy, Edward: Chappaquiddick car accident, xvii, 6, 84, 85, 124, 125, 146; and the Democrats, 156; Rabbit appropriates Kennedy's tragedy, 125, 126, 156
Kennedy, John, 11, 50, 82, 84, 86, 91, 93, 157
Khomeini, 127, 131, 139
King,Jr., Martin Luther, 94, 103
Kruppenbach, xi, 34, 43
Krushchev, Nikita, 46

Lama (see Dalai Lama)
Lathrop Kathleen, 30, 31, 37, 63, 104, 117, 140-142, 152, 154, 158
LBJ (see Johnson, Lyndon)
Lemmon, Jack, 133
Le Pellec, Yves, 144, 158
Lincoln, Abraham, 21, 96, 97, 109
Lombardi, Vince, 59

MacMillan, Harold, xiii, 6, 40, 41, 46, 48, 50, 146
Macnaughton, William, 36, 158
MacVeagh, Lincoln, 89
Mailer, Norman, 5
Malcolm X, 94, 99-103, 111
Mallon, Thomas, 62
Manuscripts (of the Rabbit Trilogy), 60, 72

Markle, Joyce, xi, 11, 18, 19, 21-23, 31, 37

Marshfield, Tom, xi

Marx, Karl, 99

McCarthyism, 48-50, 88

Melanie, 125, 134, 136, 138 *Mim,* 70, 75, 90, 91, 96, 99, 107-109

Morrow, Lance, 137, 142

Murkett (see **Webb Murkett**)

NAACP, 111

Nehru, Jawaharlal, 41

Nelson: reactionary, xiv; Nelson's conflicts with his father, 7, 114, 115, 116, 122, 126, 127, 148; Nelson seen as a stormy sky, 28; Rabbit imagines a life without Nelson, 35; Nelson and Rabbit's views on Vietnam, 58; Nelson and Jill, 78; Nelson falls asleep during the moon landing, 83; Nelson and Mr. Springer talk about Kennedy's accident, 85; at the Greek restaurant with Rabbit, Stavros, and Janice, 88; Nelson and the ideological spectrum, 99; living with his grandparents, 107; working at Springer Motors, 121, 122; at Nelson's wedding, 122; replacing Stavros at the lot, 123; Nelson and Melanie, 125; Nelson's portrayal of Rabbit as a rebel, 127; discussing the Soviet invasion of Afghanistan with Rabbit, 131, 132; Nelson's racism, 135, 136; Nelson imitates his father, 140; Nelson and the hostage crisis, 148; Nixon, Richard: and Rabbit, xviii; and the silent majority, 76, 147; Nixon's credit hunting, 82, 84; Nixon and Vietnam, 87; Nixon and Skeeter, 104; the Nixon Administration, 117

Novak, Michael, xi, 59, 74, 145, 158

Oates Joyce C., xv

Pajasek, 102, 103

Panthers (Black Panthers), 94, 104, 111

Peggy (see **Fosnacht**)

Phillips, Kevin, 146, 158

Plato, 153

Pope John Paul II, 6, 124, 128-132

Pru, 126, 135, 136

Regan, R.A., 24-26

Rogin, Richard, 158

Ronnie (see **Harrison**)

Roosevelt, Franklin D., 24, 84, 86, 93, 125

Ruth: Rabbit's disregard of Ruth, 18; Rabbit's indecision about Ruth, 21; Ruth's lifestyle, 32, 42; sees Rabbit as the best lover, 44; jealous of Eccles and Mrs. Smith, 45; Ruth vulgarizes Rabbit's experience in the army, 53, 54; sees Rabbit as a fighter, 55, 56; Ruth and the need to win, 59; Ruth laughs at Rabbit's joke, 63, 64; Rabbit's dislike of Ruth's use of cosmetics, 68; Ruth rejects Rabbit, 75; Ruth as a good cook, 148; Ruth as a housewife, 149 Samuels, Charles T., 156, 157

Schumacher, E. F., 140

Seale, Bobby, 104

Skeeter: and the Vietnam war, 22, 79, 98; Skeeter is not the Harry of the sixties, 22; revolutionary, 23, 28, 135, 138, 150; Skeeter and the ideological spectrum, 23, 98-100, 136; Skeeter and the black protest, 29, 51, 93-100, 103, 104, 109; Skeeter and the American need to win, 59; Skeeter as Rabbit's reality instructor, 75, 123, 126; Skeeter as drug pusher, 79; Skeeter's idea of justice, 79; Skeeter helped by Rabbit, 80, 102, 103; Skeeter against the system, 94, 95, 99, 100, 105, 116, 136, 150; Skeeter sees Rabbit as the white establishment, 96-98, 101, 136; Skeeter and Nixon, 104; Skeeter and Robert Williams,

Skeeter: continued
104; Skeeter and the Black
Panthers, 104; Skeeter's alliance
with Jill, 106; Skeeter in
MS # 1020, 107, 111, 112; Nelson's
traumatic memories of Skeeter,
127; Skeeter neutralized by the
establishment, 138; Skeeter as a
ghostly presence, 149 *Smith, Mrs.*:
cold and utilitarian, 44; in love
with Rabbit, 45; the war motif,
57-59, 91
SNCC, 94, 111
Soupy, xi, 33, 123
Springer, Mr.: self-annihilation, 56; as
a reality instructor, 75; his views
on the Ted Kennedy accident,
84-86; his views on FDR, 93; his
position in the ideological
spectrum, 99;
Springer, Mrs.: pushy, 116, 123;
reviving her husband's pro-
Republican views, 125; her racism,
135, 136
Sragow, Michael, 2
Stavros, Charlie: Stavros and the
ideological spectrum, xvii, 23, 79,
88, 95, 99, 107, 120, 149, 152;
Stavros as reality instructor, 75, 88,
89, 91, 101; seen as a "foreigner,"
76, 78, 89; affair with Janice, 77,
108; what Stavros thinks of
Rabbit's flag, 88; his views on
Vietnam, 89; what he thinks
Rabbit's problems are, 91, 101;
what he thinks of Johnson and
Kennedy, 93; Stavros and Skeeter,
95, 98; Stavros's "affair" with
Mim, 108; the credibility of
Stavros's words, 110, 141; his views
on the oil crisis, 119-121, 128;
replaced by Nelson at the lot, 123;

his views on the Ted Kennedy
accident, 125; what he thinks of
the hostage crisis, 128; what he
thinks of the pope, 129, 130; on
America's helplessness, 131; on the
system's absorption of the hippies,
138; Stavros and Rabbit's
nightmare, 139
Stern, Fritz, 155, 158

Taft-Hartley Act, 50
Taylor, Larry, 67
Ted Kennedy, (see **Kennedy,
Edward**)
Thorburn, David, 36
Tothero: as Rabbit's haven, 7, 39, 40,
42, 55, 56, 63, 65, 66, 114; the
Hamiltons' heaven-sent
messenger, 12, 14, 15; Tothero and
the sacred rules and virtues, 34,
45, 62; Tothero and the importance
of winning, 55, 56, 59; Tothero and
the war motif, 59, 60; Tothero and
Rabbit's job, 64, 66, 114
Truman, Harry, 11, 49, 55, 88, 157

Uphaus Suzanne Henning, xi, 11,
26, 27, 28, 37

Vargo, Edward, xi, xix, 11, 18, 19, 26,
37
Vaughn, Phillip, xix, 22, 28, 29, 30,
37
Vidal, Gore, 76

Walcutt, Charles C., 62
Warren, Donald, xviii, 43, 65, 77, 122
Webb Murkett, 6, 127-129
White, Hayden, 5, 10, 156, 159
Williams, Robert, 103, 104
Wilson, Charles, 49, 52, 71, 126

Karen Marguerite Radell

AFFIRMATION IN A MORAL WASTELAND
A Comparison of Ford Madox and Graham Greene

American University Studies: Series IV (English Language and Literature).
Vol. 54
ISBN 0-8204-0499-3   243 pages   hardback US $ 33.00*

*Recommended price – alterations reserved

This study broadens the aesthetic horizons of both Ford and Greene criticism and at the same time facilitates a full appreciation of their respective positions in modern letters. Ford criticism is still hampered by the tendency to view him as a late Victorian/Edwardian spokesman, in much the same way that Greene criticism is often hampered by a preoccupation with Greene's Catholicism.
Radell examines in detail certain representative works of each author and discusses Ford's overlooked non-fiction, as well as the artistic relationship between Ford and Greene. This study also shares letters from Greene and his comments made during a January 1982 interview with him.

«... Karen Radell's work ... seems to me to open a whole world of scholarly investigation .... It is a most valuable contribution indeed.»
(John L. Carey, Bloomfield College)

PETER LANG PUBLISHING, INC.
62 West 45th Street
USA – New York, NY 10036

Benjamin Newman

SEARCHING FOR THE FIGURE IN THE CARPET IN THE TALES OF HENRY JAMES
Reflections of an Ordinary Reader

American University Studies: Series IV (English Language and Literature).
Vol. 49
ISBN 0-8204-0442-X   200 pages   hardback US $ 39.00*

*Recommended price – alterations reserved

Undertaken as if by an ordinary reader concentrating upon fundamentals of feeling and thought in the tales of Henry James, this study by Professor Newman is a probing, questioning, analytical search for the Jamesian figure, for the ultimate messages communicated by James, about his life and the world. Joining this distinctive perspective, a personalized style, and solid scholarly exploration, the book probes for meaning behind visions and metaphors over an expanse from *Daisy Miller* to *The Jolly Corner*, from the early years to the closing stage, the final years of recollection. As the odyssey progresses, its findings confirm for the author his conviction that there is indeed a «figure in the carpet», a consistent, coherent, and unified vision of James's life and of man's that runs through the tales, but modified in certain ways as the years passed. It is a complex design which, once uncovered and grasped, enables the reader to penetrate James's symbolic system, to resolve the so-called ambiguities and obscurities so often ascribed to him, and to interpret with confidence what James is saying to us as he writes about life and society, about art and personal passion and death.

PETER LANG PUBLISHING, INC.
62 West 45th Street
USA – New York, NY 10036